HAMLET
PRINCE OF DENMARK

HAMLET
PRINCE OF DENMARK

BLOOMSBURY

This edition first published in Great Britain 2000

Cover art © Miramax Films

Bloomsbury Publishing plc, 38 Soho Square, London W1V 5DF

A CIP catalogue record for this book
is available from the British Library

ISBN 0 7475 4913 3

10 9 8 7 6 5 4 3 2 1

Typeset by Hewer Text Ltd, Edinburgh
Printed in Great Britain by Clays Ltd, St Ives plc

LIST OF CHARACTERS

HAMLET, *Prince of Denmark*
CLAUDIUS, *King of Denmark, Hamlet's uncle*
GERTRUDE, *Queen of Denmark, Hamlet's mother*
GHOST *of Hamlet's father, the former King of Denmark*
POLONIUS, *counsellor to the king*
LAERTES, *his son*
OPHELIA, *his daughter*
REYNALDO, *his servant*
HORATIO, *Hamlet's friend and fellow-student*
MARCELLUS ⎫
BARNARDO   ⎬ *officers of the watch*
FRANCISCO ⎭
VOLTEMAND ⎫ *ambassadors to Norway*
CORNELIUS   ⎭
ROSENCRANTZ ⎫ *former schoolfellows of Hamlet*
GUILDENSTERN ⎭
FORTINBRAS, *Prince of Norway*
CAPTAIN *in the Norwegian army*
First PLAYER
Other PLAYERS
OSRIC ⎫
LORD   ⎬ *courtiers*
GENTLEMAN ⎭
First CLOWN, *a gravedigger and sexton*
Second CLOWN, *his assistant*
SAILOR
MESSENGER
PRIEST
English AMBASSADOR
LORDS, ATTENDANTS, SAILORS, SOLDIERS, GUARDS

SCENE: *The Danish royal palace at Elsinore*

HAMLET
PRINCE OF DENMARK

1.1 *Enter* BARNARDO *and* FRANCISCO, *two sentinels*

BARNARDO Who's there?
FRANCISCO Nay answer me. Stand and unfold yourself.
BARNARDO Long live the king!
FRANCISCO Barnardo?
BARNARDO He.   5
FRANCISCO You come most carefully upon your hour.
BARNARDO 'Tis now struck twelve, get thee to bed Francisco.
FRANCISCO For this relief much thanks, 'tis bitter cold
        And I am sick at heart.
BARNARDO Have you had quiet guard?
FRANCISCO   Not a mouse stirring.   10
BARNARDO Well, good night.
        If you do meet Horatio and Marcellus,
        The rivals of my watch, bid them make haste.
FRANCISCO I think I hear them.

        Enter HORATIO *and* MARCELLUS

        Stand ho! Who is there?
HORATIO Friends to this ground.
MARCELLUS   And liegemen to the Dane.   15
FRANCISCO Give you good night.
MARCELLUS   Oh farewell honest soldier,
        Who hath relieved you?
FRANCISCO   Barnardo hath my place.
        Give you good night.   *Exit Francisco*
MARCELLUS   Holla, Barnardo!
BARNARDO   Say,
        What, is Horatio there?
HORATIO   A piece of him.
BARNARDO Welcome Horatio, welcome good Marcellus.   20
MARCELLUS What, has this thing appeared again tonight?
BARNARDO I have seen nothing.
MARCELLUS Horatio says 'tis but our fantasy,
        And will not let belief take hold of him
        Touching this dreaded sight, twice seen of us.   25

Therefore I have entreated him along
With us to watch the minutes of this night,
That if again this apparition come
He may approve our eyes, and speak to it.

HORATIO Tush, tush, 'twill not appear.

BARNARDO   Sit down awhile,   30
And let us once again assail your ears,
That are so fortified against our story,
What we two nights have seen.

HORATIO   Well, sit we down,
And let us hear Barnardo speak of this.

BARNARDO Last night of all,   35
When yond same star that's westward from the pole
Had made his course t'illume that part of heaven
Where now it burns, Marcellus and myself,
The bell then beating one –

Enter GHOST

MARCELLUS Peace, break thee off. Look where it comes again.   40
BARNARDO In the same figure, like the king that's dead.
MARCELLUS Thou art a scholar, speak to it Horatio.
BARNARDO Looks a not like the king? Mark it Horatio.
HORATIO Most like. It harrows me with fear and wonder.
BARNARDO It would be spoke to.
MARCELLUS   Question it Horatio.   45
HORATIO What art thou that usurp'st this time of night,
Together with that fair and warlike form
In which the majesty of buried Denmark
Did sometimes march? By heaven I charge thee speak.
MARCELLUS It is offended.
BARNARDO   See, it stalks away.   50
HORATIO Stay! Speak, speak, I charge thee speak!

Exit Ghost

MARCELLUS 'Tis gone and will not answer.
BARNARDO How now Horatio? you tremble and look pale.
Is not this something more than fantasy?
What think you on't?   55
HORATIO Before my God, I might not this believe
Without the sensible and true avouch
Of mine own eyes.
MARCELLUS   Is it not like the king?

HORATIO As thou art to thyself.

          Such was the very armour he had on   60
          When he th'ambitious Norway combated;
          So frowned he once, when in an angry parle
          He smote the sledded Polacks on the ice.
          'Tis strange.

MARCELLUS Thus twice before, and jump at this dead hour,   65
          With martial stalk hath he gone by our watch.

HORATIO In what particular thought to work I know not,
          But in the gross and scope of mine opinion
          This bodes some strange eruption to our state.

MARCELLUS Good now sit down, and tell me he that knows,   70
          Why this same strict and most observant watch
          So nightly toils the subject of the land,
          And why such daily cast of brazen cannon,
          And foreign mart for implements of war,
          Why such impress of shipwrights, whose sore task   75
          Does not divide the Sunday from the week.
          What might be toward, that this sweaty haste
          Doth make the night joint-labourer with the day?
          Who is't that can inform me?

HORATIO   That can I –
          At least the whisper goes so. Our last king,   80
          Whose image even but now appeared to us,
          Was as you know by Fortinbras of Norway,
          Thereto pricked on by a most emulate pride,
          Dared to the combat; in which our valiant Hamlet –
          For so this side of our known world esteemed him –   85
          Did slay this Fortinbras; who by a sealed compact,
          Well ratified by law and heraldy,
          Did forfeit (with his life) all those his lands
          Which he stood seized of, to the conqueror;
          Against the which a moiety competent   90
          Was gagèd by our king, which had returned
          To the inheritance of Fortinbras
          Had he been vanquisher; as by the same comart
          And carriage of the article design,
          His fell to Hamlet. Now sir, young Fortinbras,   95
          Of unimprovèd mettle hot and full,
          Hath in the skirts of Norway here and there
          Sharked up a list of landless resolutes

For food and diet to some enterprise
That hath a stomach in't; which is no other,   100
As it doth well appear unto our state,
But to recover of us by strong hand
And terms compulsatory those foresaid lands
So by his father lost. And this, I take it,
Is the main motive of our preparations,   105
The source of this our watch, and the chief head
Of this post-haste and romage in the land.

[BARNARDO I think it be no other but e'en so.
Well may it sort that this portentous figure
Comes armèd through our watch so like the king   110
That was and is the question of these wars.

HORATIO A mote it is to trouble the mind's eye.
In the most high and palmy state of Rome,
A little ere the mightiest Julius fell,
The graves stood tenantless and the sheeted dead   115
Did squeak and gibber in the Roman streets;
As stars with trains of fire, and dews of blood,
Disasters in the sun; and the moist star,
Upon whose influence Neptune's empire stands,
Was sick almost to doomsday with eclipse.   120
And even the like precurse of feared events,
As harbingers preceding still the fates
And prologue to the omen coming on,
Have heaven and earth together demonstrated
Unto our climatures and countrymen.]   125

Enter GHOST

But soft, behold, lo where it comes again!
I'll cross it though it blast me. Stay, illusion.
It spreads his arms
If thou hast any sound or use of voice,
Speak to me.
If there be any good thing to be done   130
That may to thee do ease, and grace to me,
Speak to me.
If thou art privy to thy country's fate,
Which happily foreknowing may avoid,
Oh speak.   135
Or if thou hast uphoarded in thy life

Extorted treasure in the womb of earth,
For which they say you spirits oft walk in death,   *The cock crows*
Speak of it. Stay and speak! Stop it Marcellus.

MARCELLUS Shall I strike at it with my partisan?   140

HORATIO Do if it will not stand.

BARNARDO   'Tis here.

HORATIO   'Tis here.

MARCELLUS 'Tis gone.

                                                    Exit Ghost

We do it wrong being so majestical
To offer it the show of violence,
For it is as the air invulnerable,   145
And our vain blows malicious mockery.

BARNARDO It was about to speak when the cock crew.

HORATIO And then it started like a guilty thing
Upon a fearful summons. I have heard,
The cock, that is the trumpet to the morn,   150
Doth with his lofty and shrill-sounding throat
Awake the god of day; and at his warning,
Whether in sea or fire, in earth or air,
Th'extravagant and erring spirit hies
To his confine. And of the truth herein   155
This present object made probation.

MARCELLUS It faded on the crowing of the cock.
Some say that ever 'gainst that season comes
Wherein our Saviour's birth is celebrated,
This bird of dawning singeth all night long,   160
And then, they say, no spirit dare stir abroad,
The nights are wholesome, then no planets strike,
No fairy takes, nor witch hath power to charm,
So hallowed and so gracious is that time.

HORATIO So have I heard, and do in part believe it.   165
But look, the morn in russet mantle clad
Walks o'er the dew of yon high eastward hill.
Break we our watch up, and by my advice
Let us impart what we have seen tonight
Unto young Hamlet, for upon my life   170
This spirit, dumb to us, will speak to him.
Do you consent we shall acquaint him with it,
As needful in our loves, fitting our duty?

MARCELLUS Let's do't I pray, and I this morning know

Where we shall find him most conveniently.   175

Exeunt

1.2 *Flourish. Enter* CLAUDIUS *King of Denmark,* GERTRUDE *the Queen,*
HAMLET, POLONIUS, LAERTES, OPHELIA, [VOLTEMAND, CORNELIUS,] LORDS
attendant

CLAUDIUS Though yet of Hamlet our dear brother's death
    The memory be green, and that it us befitted
    To bear our hearts in grief, and our whole kingdom
    To be contracted in one brow of woe,
    Yet so far hath discretion fought with nature   5
    That we with wisest sorrow think on him,
    Together with remembrance of ourselves.
    Therefore our sometime sister, now our queen,
    Th'imperial jointress to this warlike state,
    Have we, as 'twere with a defeated joy,   10
    With one auspicious and one dropping eye,
    With mirth in funeral and with dirge in marriage,
    In equal scale weighing delight and dole,
    Taken to wife; nor have we herein barred
    Your better wisdoms, which have freely gone   15
    With this affair along – for all, our thanks.
    Now follows that you know: young Fortinbras,
    Holding a weak supposal of our worth,
    Or thinking by our late dear brother's death
    Our state to be disjoint and out of frame,   20
    Colleaguèd with this dream of his advantage,
    He hath not failed to pester us with message
    Importing the surrender of those lands
    Lost by his father, with all bands of law,
    To our most valiant brother. So much for him.   25
    Now for ourself and for this time of meeting
    Thus much the business is: we have here writ
    To Norway, uncle of young Fortinbras,
    Who, impotent and bed-rid, scarcely hears
    Of this his nephew's purpose, to suppress   30
    His further gait herein, in that the levies,
    The lists, and full proportions, are all made
    Out of his subject; and we here dispatch

You, good Cornelius, and you, Voltemand,
For bearers of this greeting to old Norway,   35
Giving to you no further personal power
To business with the king, more than the scope
Of these dilated articles allow.
Farewell, and let your haste commend your duty.

CORNELIUS ⎫ In that and all things will we show our duty.   40
VOLTEMAND ⎭

CLAUDIUS We doubt it nothing, heartily farewell.

                                Exeunt Voltemand and Cornelius

And now Laertes, what's the news with you?
You told us of some suit, what is't Laertes?
You cannot speak of reason to the Dane
And lose your voice. What wouldst thou beg Laertes,   45
That shall not be my offer, not thy asking?
The head is not more native to the heart,
The hand more instrumental to the mouth,
Than is the throne of Denmark to thy father.
What wouldst thou have Laertes?

LAERTES   My dread lord,   50
Your leave and favour to return to France,
From whence though willingly I came to Denmark
To show my duty in your coronation,
Yet now I must confess, that duty done,
My thoughts and wishes bend again toward France,   55
And bow them to your gracious leave and pardon.

CLAUDIUS Have you your father's leave? What says Polonius?

POLONIUS He hath my lord wrung from me my slow leave
By laboursome petition, and at last
Upon his will I sealed my hard consent.   60
I do beseech you give him leave to go.

CLAUDIUS Take thy fair hour Laertes, time be thine,
And thy best graces spend it at thy will.
But now my cousin Hamlet, and my son –

HAMLET (*Aside*) A little more than kin, and less than kind.   65

CLAUDIUS How is it that the clouds still hang on you?

HAMLET Not so my lord, I am too much i'th'sun.

GERTRUDE Good Hamlet cast thy nighted colour off,
And let thine eye look like a friend on Denmark.
Do not forever with thy vailèd lids   70
Seek for thy noble father in the dust.

Thou know'st 'tis common, all that lives must die,
Passing through nature to eternity.
HAMLET Ay madam, it is common.
GERTRUDE   If it be,
Why seems it so particular with thee?   75
HAMLET Seems madam? nay it is, I know not seems.
'Tis not alone my inky cloak, good mother,
Nor customary suits of solemn black,
Nor windy suspiration of forced breath,
No, nor the fruitful river in the eye,   80
Nor the dejected haviour of the visage,
Together with all forms, moods, shapes of grief,
That can denote me truly. These indeed seem,
For they are actions that a man might play,
But I have that within which passes show –   85
These but the trappings and the suits of woe.
CLAUDIUS 'Tis sweet and commendable in your nature Hamlet,
To give these mourning duties to your father;
But you must know, your father lost a father,
That father lost, lost his, and the survivor bound   90
In filial obligation for some term
To do obsequious sorrow; but to persever
In obstinate condolement is a course
Of impious stubbornness, 'tis unmanly grief,
It shows a will most incorrect to heaven,   95
A heart unfortified, a mind impatient,
An understanding simple and unschooled.
For what we know must be, and is as common
As any the most vulgar thing to sense,
Why should we in our peevish opposition   100
Take it to heart? Fie, 'tis a fault to heaven,
A fault against the dead, a fault to nature,
To reason most absurd, whose common theme
Is death of fathers, and who still hath cried,
From the first corse till he that died today,   105
'This must be so.' We pray you throw to earth
This unprevailing woe, and think of us
As of a father, for let the world take note
You are the most immediate to our throne,
And with no less nobility of love   110
Than that which dearest father bears his son,

Do I impart toward you. For your intent
In going back to school in Wittenberg,
It is most retrograde to our desire,
And we beseech you bend you to remain   115
Here in the cheer and comfort of our eye,
Our chiefest courtier, cousin, and our son.

GERTRUDE Let not thy mother lose her prayers Hamlet.
I pray thee stay with us, go not to Wittenberg.

HAMLET I shall in all my best obey you madam.   120

CLAUDIUS Why, 'tis a loving and a fair reply.
Be as ourself in Denmark. Madam, come.
This gentle and unforced accord of Hamlet
Sits smiling to my heart, in grace whereof,
No jocund health that Denmark drinks today   125
But the great cannon to the clouds shall tell,
And the king's rouse the heaven shall bruit again,
Re-speaking earthly thunder. Come away.

Flourish. Exeunt all but Hamlet

HAMLET O that this too too solid flesh would melt,
Thaw and resolve itself into a dew,   130
Or that the Everlasting had not fixed
His canon 'gainst self-slaughter. O God, God,
How weary, stale, flat and unprofitable
Seem to me all the uses of this world!
Fie on't, ah fie, 'tis an unweeded garden   135
That grows to seed, things rank and gross in nature
Possess it merely. That it should come to this!
But two months dead – nay not so much, not two –
So excellent a king, that was to this
Hyperion to a satyr, so loving to my mother   140
That he might not beteem the winds of heaven
Visit her face too roughly – heaven and earth,
Must I remember? why, she would hang on him
As if increase of appetite had grown
By what it fed on, and yet within a month –   145
Let me not think on't; frailty, thy name is woman –
A little month, or ere those shoes were old
With which she followed my poor father's body
Like Niobe, all tears, why she, even she –
O God, a beast that wants discourse of reason   150
Would have mourned longer – married with my uncle,

My father's brother, but no more like my father
Than I to Hercules – within a month,
Ere yet the salt of most unrighteous tears
Had left the flushing in her gallèd eyes,   155
She married. Oh most wicked speed, to post
With such dexterity to incestuous sheets.
It is not, nor it cannot come to good.
But break, my heart, for I must hold my tongue.

Enter HORATIO, MARCELLUS *and* BARNARDO

HORATIO Hail to your lordship.
HAMLET   I am glad to see you well.   160
    Horatio – or I do forget myself.
HORATIO The same, my lord, and your poor servant ever.
HAMLET Sir, my good friend, I'll change that name with you.
    And what make you from Wittenberg, Horatio?
    Marcellus.   165
MARCELLUS My good lord.
HAMLET I am very glad to see you. (*To Barnardo*) Good even sir.
    But what in faith make you from Wittenberg.
HORATIO A truant disposition, good my lord.
HAMLET I would not hear your enemy say so,   170
    Nor shall you do my ear that violence
    To make it truster of your own report
    Against yourself. I know you are no truant.
    But what is your affair in Elsinore?
    We'll teach you to drink deep ere you depart.   175
HORATIO My lord, I came to see your father's funeral.
HAMLET I pray thee do not mock me fellow student,
    I think it was to see my mother's wedding.
HORATIO Indeed my lord, it followed hard upon.
HAMLET Thrift, thrift, Horatio. The funeral baked meats   180
    Did coldly furnish forth the marriage tables.
    Would I had met my dearest foe in heaven
    Or ever I had seen that day, Horatio.
    My father, methinks I see my father –
HORATIO Where my lord?
HAMLET   In my mind's eye, Horatio.   185
HORATIO I saw him once, a was a goodly king.
HAMLET A was a man, take him for all in all.

	I shall not look upon his like again.	
HORATIO	My lord, I think I saw him yesternight.	
HAMLET	Saw? Who?	190
HORATIO	My lord, the king your father.	
HAMLET	The king my father!	

HORATIO Season your admiration for a while
        With an attent ear, till I may deliver
        Upon the witness of these gentlemen
        This marvel to you.
HAMLET   For God's love let me hear.   195
HORATIO Two nights together had these gentlemen,
        Marcellus and Barnardo, on their watch
        In the dead waste and middle of the night,
        Been thus encountered. A figure like your father,
        Armèd at point exactly, cap-a-pe,   200
        Appears before them, and with solemn march
        Goes slow and stately by them. Thrice he walked
        By their oppressed and fear-surprisèd eyes
        Within his truncheon's length, whilst they, distilled
        Almost to jelly with the act of fear,   205
        Stand dumb and speak not to him. This to me
        In dreadful secrecy impart they did,
        And I with them the third night kept the watch,
        Where, as they had delivered, both in time,
        Form of the thing, each word made true and good,   210
        The apparition comes. I knew your father,
        These hands are not more like.
HAMLET   But where was this?
MARCELLUS My lord, upon the platform where we watched.
HAMLET Did you not speak to it?
HORATIO   My lord, I did,
        But answer made it none. Yet once methought   215
        It lifted up it head and did address
        Itself to motion like as it would speak;
        But even then the morning cock crew loud,
        And at the sound it shrunk in haste away
        And vanished from our sight.
HAMLET   'Tis very strange.   220
HORATIO As I do live my honoured lord 'tis true,
        And we did think it writ down in our duty
        To let you know of it.

HAMLET Indeed, indeed sirs, but this troubles me.
   Hold you the watch tonight?
MARCELLUS }
BARNARDO }   We do, my lord.   225
HAMLET Armed say you?
MARCELLUS }
BARNARDO }   Armed my lord.
HAMLET   From top to toe?
MARCELLUS }
BARNARDO } My lord, from head to foot.
HAMLET Then saw you not his face?
HORATIO Oh yes my lord, he wore his beaver up.
HAMLET What, looked he frowningly?   230
HORATIO A countenance more in sorrow than in anger.
HAMLET Pale, or red?
HORATIO Nay very pale.
HAMLET   And fixed his eyes upon you?
HORATIO Most constantly.
HAMLET   I would I had been there.
HORATIO It would have much amazed you.   235
HAMLET Very like, very like. Stayed it long?
HORATIO While one with moderate haste might tell a hundred.
MARCELLUS }
BARNARDO } Longer, longer.
HORATIO Not when I saw't.
HAMLET   His beard was grizzled, no?
HORATIO It was as I have seen it in his life,   240
   A sable silvered.
HAMLET   I will watch tonight,
   Perchance 'twill walk again.
HORATIO   I warrant it will.
HAMLET If it assume my noble father's person,
   I'll speak to it though hell itself should gape
   And bid me hold my peace. I pray you all,   245
   If you have hitherto concealed this sight,
   Let it be tenable in your silence still,
   And whatsomever else shall hap tonight,
   Give it an understanding but no tongue.
   I will requite your loves. So fare you well: 250
   Upon the platform 'twixt eleven and twelve
   I'll visit you.

ALL   Our duty to your honour.
HAMLET Your loves, as mine to you. Farewell.

> *Exeunt all but Hamlet*

My father's spirit, in arms! All is not well.
I doubt some foul play. Would the night were come.   255
Till then sit still my soul. Foul deeds will rise
Though all the earth o'erwhelm them to men's eyes.   *Exit*

1.3 *Enter* LAERTES *and* OPHELIA *his sister*

LAERTES My necessaries are embarked, farewell.
And sister, as the winds give benefit
And convoy is assistant, do not sleep
But let me hear from you.
OPHELIA   Do you doubt that?
LAERTES For Hamlet, and the trifling of his favour,   5
Hold it a fashion, and a toy in blood,
A violet in the youth of primy nature,
Forward, not permanent, sweet, not lasting,
The perfume and suppliance of a minute,
No more.
OPHELIA   No more but so?
LAERTES   Think it no more.   10
For nature crescent does not grow alone
In thews and bulk, but as this temple waxes
The inward service of the mind and soul
Grows wide withal. Perhaps he loves you now,
And now no soil nor cautel doth besmirch   15
The virtue of his will; but you must fear,
His greatness weighed, his will is not his own,
For he himself is subject to his birth.
He may not, as unvalued persons do,
Carve for himself, for on his choice depends   20
The sanctity and health of this whole state,
And therefore must his choice be circumscribed
Unto the voice and yielding of that body
Whereof he is the head. Then if he says he loves you,
It fits your wisdom so far to believe it   25
As he in his peculiar sect and force
May give his saying deed, which is no further

Than the main voice of Denmark goes withal.
Then weigh what loss your honour may sustain
If with too credent ear you list his songs,   30
Or lose your heart, or your chaste treasure open
To his unmastered importunity.
Fear it Ophelia, fear it my dear sister,
And keep you in the rear of your affection,
Out of the shot and danger of desire.   35
The chariest maid is prodigal enough
If she unmask her beauty to the moon.
Virtue itself scapes not calumnious strokes.
The canker galls the infants of the spring
Too oft before their buttons be disclosed,   40
And in the morn and liquid dew of youth
Contagious blastments are most imminent.
Be wary then, best safety lies in fear:
Youth to itself rebels, though none else near.

OPHELIA I shall th'effect of this good lesson keep   45
And As watchman to my heart. But good my brother,
Do not as some ungracious pastors do,
Show me the steep and thorny way to heaven,
Whiles like a puffed and reckless libertine
Himself the primrose path of dalliance treads,   50
And recks not his own rede.

LAERTES   Oh fear me not.

Enter POLONIUS

I stay too long – But here my father comes.
A double blessing is a double grace;
Occasion smiles upon a second leave.

POLONIUS Yet here Laertes? Aboard, aboard for shame!   55
The wind sits in the shoulder of your sail,
And you are stayed for. There, my blessing with thee,
And these few precepts in thy memory
Look thou character. Give thy thoughts no tongue,
Nor any unproportioned thought his act.   60
Be thou familiar, but by no means vulgar.
Those friends thou hast, and their adoption tried,
Grapple them unto thy soul with hoops of steel,
But do not dull thy palm with entertainment
Of each new-hatched, unfledged courage. Beware   65

Of entrance to a quarrel, but being in,
Bear't that th'opposèd may beware of thee.
Give every man thy ear, but few thy voice;
Take each man's censure, but reserve thy judgement.
Costly thy habit as thy purse can buy,   70
But not expressed in fancy: rich, not gaudy.
For the apparel oft proclaims the man,
And they in France of the best rank and station
Are of a most select and generous chief in that.
Neither a borrower nor a lender be,   75
For loan oft loses both itself and friend,
And borrowing dulls the edge of husbandry.
This above all, to thine own self be true,
And it must follow, as the night the day,
Thou canst not then be false to any man.   80
Farewell, my blessing season this in thee.

LAERTES Most humbly do I take my leave, my lord.

POLONIUS The time invites you. Go, your servants tend.

LAERTES Farewell Ophelia, and remember well
    What I have said to you.

OPHELIA   'Tis in my memory locked,   85
    And you yourself shall keep the key of it.

LAERTES Farewell.   *Exit Laertes*

POLONIUS What is't Ophelia he hath said to you?

OPHELIA So please you, something touching the Lord Hamlet.

POLONIUS Marry, well bethought.   90
    'Tis told me he hath very oft of late
    Given private time to you, and you yourself
    Have of your audience been most free and bounteous.
    If it be so, as so 'tis put on me,
    And that in way of caution, I must tell you   95
    You do not understand yourself so clearly
    As it behooves my daughter, and your honour.
    What is between you? Give me up the truth.

OPHELIA He hath my lord of late made many tenders
    Of his affection to me.   100

POLONIUS Affection? Puh! You speak like a green girl,
    Unsifted in such perilous circumstance.
    Do you believe his tenders as you call them?

OPHELIA I do not know my lord what I should think.

POLONIUS Marry I'll teach you. Think yourself a baby   105

That you have tane these tenders for true pay,
Which are not sterling. Tender yourself more dearly,
Or – not to crack the wind of the poor phrase,
Roaming it thus – you'll tender me a fool.

OPHELIA   My lord, he hath importuned me with love   110
In honourable fashion.

POLONIUS   Ay, fashion you may call it. Go to, go to.

OPHELIA   And hath given countenance to his speech, my lord,
With almost all the holy vows of heaven.

POLONIUS   Ay, springes to catch woodcocks. I do know,   115
When the blood burns, how prodigal the soul
Lends the tongue vows. These blazes daughter,
Giving more light than heat, extinct in both
Even in their promise as it is a-making,
You must not take for fire. From this time   120
Be something scanter of your maiden presence.
Set your entreatments at a higher rate
Than a command to parley. For Lord Hamlet,
Believe so much in him, that he is young
And with a larger tedder may he walk   125
Than may be given you. In few Ophelia,
Do not believe his vows, for they are brokers,
Not of that dye which their investments show,
But mere implorators of unholy suits,
Breathing like sanctified and pious bonds,   130
The better to beguile. This is for all:
I would not in plain terms from this time forth
Have you so slander any moment leisure
As to give words or talk with the Lord Hamlet.
Look to't I charge you. Come your ways.   135

OPHELIA   I shall obey, my lord.

Exeunt

[1.4] *Enter* HAMLET, HORATIO *and* MARCELLUS

HAMLET   The air bites shrewdly, it is very cold.

HORATIO   It is a nipping and an eager air.

HAMLET   What hour now?

HORATIO   I think it lacks of twelve.

MARCELLUS   No, it is struck.

HORATIO   Indeed? I heard it not. It then draws near the season   5

Wherein the spirit held his wont to walk.
A flourish of trumpets and two pieces goes off
What does this mean, my lord?
HAMLET The king doth wake tonight and takes his rouse,
Keeps wassail, and the swaggering up-spring reels,
And as he drains his draughts of Rhenish down,   10
The kettle-drum and trumpet thus bray out
The triumph of his pledge.
HORATIO   Is it a custom?
HAMLET Ay marry is't,
But to my mind, though I am native here
And to the manner born, it is a custom   15
More honoured in the breach than the observance.
[This heavy-headed revel east and west
Makes us traduced and taxed of other nations.
They clepe us drunkards, and with swinish phrase
Soil our addition; and indeed it takes   20
From our achievements, though performed at height,
The pith and marrow of our attribute.
So, oft it chances in particular men,
That for some vicious mole of nature in them,
As in their birth, wherein they are not guilty,   25
Since nature cannot choose his origin,
By their o'ergrowth of some complexion,
Oft breaking down the pales and forts of reason,
Or by some habit that too much o'erleavens
The form of plausive manners – that these men,   30
Carrying I say the stamp of one defect,
Being nature's livery or fortune's star,
His virtues else be they as pure as grace,
As infinite as man may undergo,
Shall in the general censure take corruption   35
From that particular fault. The dram of eale
Doth all the noble substance of a doubt
To his own scandal.]

Enter GHOST

HORATIO   Look my lord, it comes!
HAMLET Angels and ministers of grace defend us!
Be thou a spirit of health, or goblin damned,   40
Bring with thee airs from heaven or blasts from hell,

Be thy intents wicked or charitable,
Thou com'st in such a questionable shape
That I will speak to thee. I'll call thee Hamlet,
King, father, royal Dane. Oh answer me.   45
Let me not burst in ignorance, but tell
Why thy canonised bones, hearsèd in death,
Have burst their cerements; why the sepulchre,
Wherein we saw thee quietly enurned,
Hath oped his ponderous and marble jaws   50
To cast thee up again. What may this mean,
That thou, dead corse, again in complete steel
Revisits thus the glimpses of the moon,
Making night hideous, and we fools of nature
So horridly to shake our disposition   55
With thoughts beyond the reaches of our souls?
Say, why is this? wherefore? What should we do?

Ghost beckons Hamlet

HORATIO It beckons you to go away with it,
  As if it some impartment did desire
  To you alone.
MARCELLUS   Look with what courteous action   60
  It wafts you to a more removèd ground.
  But do not go with it.
HORATIO   No, by no means.
HAMLET It will not speak. Then I will follow it.
HORATIO Do not my lord.
HAMLET   Why, what should be the fear?
  I do not set my life at a pin's fee,   65
  And for my soul, what can it do to that,
  Being a thing immortal as itself?
  It waves me forth again. I'll follow it.
HORATIO What if it tempt you toward the flood my lord,
  Or to the dreadful summit of the cliff   70
  That beetles o'er his base into the sea,
  And there assume some other horrible form
  Which might deprive your sovereignty of reason,
  And draw you into madness? Think of it.
  [The very place puts toys of desperation,   75
  Without more motive, into every brain
  That looks so many fathoms to the sea
  And hears it roar beneath.]

HAMLET It wafts me still. Go on, I'll follow thee.
MARCELLUS You shall not go my lord.
HAMLET   Hold off your hands.   80
HORATIO Be ruled, you shall not go.
HAMLET   My fate cries out,
    And makes each petty arture in this body
    As hardy as the Nemean lion's nerve.
    Still am I called. Unhand me gentlemen!
    By heaven I'll make a ghost of him that lets me.   85
    I say away! – Go on, I'll follow thee.

                        Exit Ghost and Hamlet

HORATIO He waxes desperate with imagination.
MARCELLUS Let's follow, 'tis not fit thus to obey him.
HORATIO Have after. To what issue will this come?
MARCELLUS Something is rotten in the state of Denmark.   90
HORATIO Heaven will direct it.
MARCELLUS   Nay let's follow him.

                             Exeunt

[1.5] *Enter* GHOST *and* HAMLET

HAMLET Whither wilt thou lead me? Speak, I'll go no further.
GHOST Mark me.
HAMLET   I will.
GHOST   My hour is almost come
    When I to sulph'rous and tormenting flames
    Must render up myself.
HAMLET   Alas poor ghost!
GHOST Pity me not, but lend thy serious hearing   5
    To what I shall unfold.
HAMLET   Speak, I am bound to hear.
GHOST So art thou to revenge, when thou shalt hear.
HAMLET What?
GHOST I am thy father's spirit,
    Doomed for a certain term to walk the night,   10
    And for the day confined to fast in fires,
    Till the foul crimes done in my days of nature
    Are burnt and purged away. But that I am forbid
    To tell the secrets of my prison house,
    I could a tale unfold whose lightest word   15

Would harrow up thy soul, freeze thy young blood,
Make thy two eyes like stars start from their spheres,
Thy knotted and combinèd locks to part
And each particular hair to stand an end
Like quills upon the fretful porpentine.   20
But this eternal blazon must not be
To ears of flesh and blood. List, list, oh list!
If thou didst ever thy dear father love –

HAMLET O God!

GHOST Revenge his foul and most unnatural murder.   25

HAMLET Murder?

GHOST Murder most foul, as in the best it is,
But this most foul, strange, and unnatural.

HAMLET Haste me to know't, that I with wings as swift
As meditation or the thoughts of love   30
May sweep to my revenge.

GHOST   I find thee apt,
And duller shouldst thou be than the fat weed
That rots itself in ease on Lethe wharf,
Wouldst thou not stir in this. Now Hamlet, hear.
'Tis given out that, sleeping in my orchard,   35
A serpent stung me. So the whole ear of Denmark
Is by a forgèd process of my death
Rankly abused; but know, thou noble youth,
The serpent that did sting thy father's life
Now wears his crown.

HAMLET   O my prophetic soul!   40
My uncle?

GHOST Ay, that incestuous, that adulterate beast,
With witchcraft of his wits, with traitorous gifts –
O wicked wit and gifts that have the power
So to seduce – won to his shameful lust   45
The will of my most seeming virtuous queen.
O Hamlet, what a falling off was there,
From me whose love was of that dignity
That it went hand in hand even with the vow
I made to her in marriage, and to decline   50
Upon a wretch whose natural gifts were poor
To those of mine.
But virtue as it never will be moved,
Though lewdness court it in a shape of heaven,

So lust, though to a radiant angel linked,   55
Will sate itself in a celestial bed,
And prey on garbage.
But soft, methinks I scent the morning air;
Brief let me be. Sleeping within my orchard,
My custom always of the afternoon,   60
Upon my secure hour thy uncle stole,
With juice of cursèd hebenon in a vial,
And in the porches of my ears did pour
The leperous distilment, whose effect
Holds such an enmity with blood of man   65
That swift as quicksilver it courses through
The natural gates and alleys of the body,
And with a sudden vigour it doth posset
And curd, like eager droppings into milk,
The thin and wholesome blood. So did it mine,   70
And a most instant tetter barked about,
Most lazar-like, with vile and loathsome crust,
All my smooth body.
Thus was I, sleeping, by a brother's hand,
Of life, of crown, of queen, at once dispatched;   75
Cut off even in the blossoms of my sin,
Unhouseled, disappointed, unaneled;
No reckoning made, but sent to my account
With all my imperfections on my head –
Oh horrible, oh horrible, most horrible!   80
If thou hast nature in thee bear it not;
Let not the royal bed of Denmark be
A couch for luxury and damnèd incest.
But howsomever thou pursues this act
Taint not thy mind, nor let thy soul contrive   85
Against thy mother aught. Leave her to heaven
And to those thorns that in her bosom lodge
To prick and sting her. Fare thee well at once.
The glow-worm shows the matin to be near,
And gins to pale his uneffectual fire.   90
Adieu, adieu, adieu. Remember me.   *Exit*

HAMLET O all you host of heaven! O earth! what else?
And shall I couple hell? Oh fie! Hold, hold, my heart,
And you my sinews grow not instant old
But bear me stiffly up. Remember thee?   95

Ay thou poor ghost, whiles memory holds a seat
In this distracted globe. Remember thee?
Yea, from the table of my memory
I'll wipe away all trivial fond records,
All saws of books, all forms, all pressures past,   100
That youth and observation copied there,
And thy commandment all alone shall live
Within the book and volume of my brain,
Unmixed with baser matter: yes, by heaven!
O most pernicious woman!   105
O villain, villain, smiling damnèd villain!
My tables – meet it is I set it down
That one may smile, and smile, and be a villain;
At least I'm sure it may be so in Denmark. [*Writing*]
So uncle, there you are. Now to my word: 110
It is 'Adieu, adieu, remember me.'
I have sworn't.

HORATIO (*Within*) My lord, my lord!
MARCELLUS (*Within*)   Lord Hamlet!

Enter HORATIO *and* MARCELLUS

HORATIO   Heavens secure him!
HAMLET So be it.
MARCELLUS Illo, ho, ho, my lord!   115
HAMLET Hillo, ho, ho, boy! Come bird, come.
MARCELLUS How is't, my noble lord?
HORATIO   What news my lord?
HAMLET Oh, wonderful!
HORATIO Good my lord, tell it.
HAMLET   No, you will reveal it.
HORATIO Not I my lord, by heaven.
MARCELLUS   Nor I my lord.   120
HAMLET How say you then, would heart of man once think it –
      But you'll be secret?
HORATIO   }
MARCELLUS   }   Ay, by heaven, my lord.
HAMLET There's ne'er a villain dwelling in all Denmark
      But he's an arrant knave.
HORATIO There needs no ghost, my lord, come from the grave,   125
      To tell us this.
HAMLET   Why right, you are i'th'right,

        And so without more circumstance at all
        I hold it fit that we shake hands and part –
        You as your business and desire shall point you,
        For every man hath business and desire,   130
        Such as it is, and for my own poor part,
        Look you, I'll go pray.

HORATIO These are but wild and whirling words, my lord.

HAMLET I'm sorry they offend you, heartily,
        Yes faith, heartily.

HORATIO   There's no offence my lord.   135

HAMLET Yes by Saint Patrick but there is Horatio,
        And much offence too. Touching this vision here,
        It is an honest ghost, that let me tell you.
        For your desire to know what is between us,
        O'ermaster't as you may. And now good friends,   140
        As you are friends, scholars, and soldiers,
        Give me one poor request.

HORATIO What is't my lord? we will.

HAMLET Never make known what you have seen tonight.

HORATIO }
MARCELLUS } My lord we will not.

HAMLET   Nay but swear't.

HORATIO   In faith   145
        My lord not I.

MARCELLUS   Nor I my lord in faith.

HAMLET Upon my sword.

MARCELLUS   We have sworn my lord already.

HAMLET Indeed, upon my sword, indeed.

GHOST Swear.   *Ghost cries under the stage*

HAMLET Ha, ha, boy, sayst thou so? art thou there truepenny?   150
        Come on, you hear this fellow in the cellarage,
        Consent to swear.

HORATIO   Propose the oath my lord.

HAMLET Never to speak of this that you have seen,
        Swear by my sword.

GHOST Swear.   155

HAMLET *Hic et ubique?* then we'll shift our ground.
        Come hither gentlemen,
        And lay your hands again upon my sword.
        Never to speak of this that you have heard,
        Swear by my sword.   160

GHOST Swear.

HAMLET Well said old mole, canst work i'th'earth so fast?
   A worthy pioneer. Once more remove, good friends.

HORATIO O day and night, but this is wondrous strange.

HAMLET And therefore as a stranger give it welcome.   165
   There are more things in heaven and earth, Horatio,
   Than are dreamt of in your philosophy.
   But come –
   Here as before, never so help you mercy,
   How strange or odd some'er I bear myself,   170
   As I perchance hereafter shall think meet
   To put an antic disposition on –
   That you at such times seeing me never shall,
   With arms encumbered thus, or this head-shake,
   Or by pronouncing of some doubtful phrase,   175
   As 'Well, well, we know,' or 'We could and if we would,'
   Or 'If we list to speak,' or 'There be and if they might,'
   Or such ambiguous giving out, to note
   That you know aught of me: this not to do,
   So grace and mercy at your most need help you,   180
   Swear.

GHOST Swear.

HAMLET Rest, rest, perturbèd spirit. So gentlemen,
   With all my love I do commend me to you,
   And what so poor a man as Hamlet is   185
   May do t'express his love and friending to you,
   God willing shall not lack. Let us go in together,
   And still your fingers on your lips I pray. –
   The time is out of joint: O cursèd spite,
   That ever I was born to set it right. –   190
   Nay come, let's go together.

              Exeunt

2.1 *Enter* POLONIUS *and* REYNALDO

POLONIUS Give him this money, and these notes, Reynaldo.

REYNALDO I will my lord.

POLONIUS You shall do marvellous wisely, good Reynaldo,
   Before you visit him, to make inquire
   Of his behaviour.

REYNALDO   My lord, I did intend it.   5
POLONIUS Marry well said, very well said. Look you sir,
            Inquire me first what Danskers are in Paris,
            And how, and who, what means, and where they keep,
            What company, at what expense; and finding
            By this encompassment and drift of question   10
            That they do know my son, come you more nearer
            Than your particular demands will touch it.
            Take you as 'twere some distant knowledge of him,
            As thus, 'I know his father and his friends,
            And in part him' – do you mark this Reynaldo?   15
REYNALDO Ay, very well, my lord.
POLONIUS 'And in part him, but' – you may say – 'not well,
            But if't be he I mean, he's very wild,
            Addicted so and so' – and there put on him
            What forgeries you please; marry, none so rank   20
            As may dishonour him, take heed of that,
            But sir, such wanton, wild, and usual slips
            As are companions noted and most known
            To youth and liberty.
REYNALDO   As gaming my lord?
POLONIUS Ay, or drinking, fencing, swearing,   25
            Quarrelling, drabbing – you may go so far.
REYNALDO My lord, that would dishonour him.
POLONIUS Faith no, as you may season it in the charge.
            You must not put another scandal on him,
            That he is open to incontinency,   30
            That's not my meaning. But breathe his faults so quaintly
            That they may seem the taints of liberty,
            The flash and outbreak of a fiery mind,
            A savageness in unreclaimèd blood,
            Of general assault.
REYNALDO   But my good lord –   35
POLONIUS Wherefore should you do this?
REYNALDO   Ay my lord,
            I would know that.
POLONIUS   Marry sir, here's my drift,
            And I believe it is a fetch of warrant.
            You laying these slight sullies on my son,
            As 'twere a thing a little soiled i'th' working,   40
            Mark you,

        Your party in converse, him you would sound,
        Having ever seen in the prenominate crimes
        The youth you breathe of guilty, be assured
        He closes with you in this consequence,   45
        'Good sir', or so, or 'friend', or 'gentleman',
        According to the phrase and the addition
        Of man and country.
REYNALDO   Very good my lord.
POLONIUS And then sir does a this – a does – what was I about to say?
    By the mass I was about to say something. Where did I leave?   50
REYNALDO At 'closes in the consequence', at 'friend, or so', and
    'gentleman'.
POLONIUS At 'closes in the consequence' – ay marry,
        He closes with you thus: 'I know the gentleman,
        I saw him yesterday, or th'other day,   55
        Or then, or then, with such or such, and as you say,
        There was a gaming, there o'ertook in's rouse,
        There falling out at tennis', or perchance,
        'I saw him enter such a house of sale' –
        Videlicet, a brothel – or so forth. See you now,   60
        Your bait of falsehood takes this carp of truth,
        And thus do we of wisdom and of reach,
        With windlasses and with assays of bias,
        By indirections find directions out.
        So, by my former lecture and advice,   65
        Shall you my son. You have me, have you not?
REYNALDO My lord, I have.
POLONIUS   God buy ye, fare ye well.
REYNALDO Good my lord.
POLONIUS Observe his inclination in yourself.
REYNALDO I shall my lord.   70
POLONIUS And let him ply his music.
REYNALDO   Well my lord.
POLONIUS Farewell.

                                            Exit Reynaldo

                        Enter OPHELIA

                How now Ophelia, what's the matter?
OPHELIA Oh my lord, my lord, I have been so affrighted.
POLONIUS With what, i'th'name of God?
OPHELIA My lord, as I was sewing in my closet,   75

Lord Hamlet with his doublet all unbraced,
No hat upon his head, his stockings fouled,
Ungartered, and down-gyvèd to his ankle,
Pale as his shirt, his knees knocking each other,
And with a look so piteous in purport   80
As if he had been loosèd out of hell
To speak of horrors – he comes before me.

POLONIUS Mad for thy love?

OPHELIA   My lord I do not know,
But truly I do fear it.

POLONIUS   What said he?

OPHELIA He took me by the wrist, and held me hard;   85
Then goes he to the length of all his arm,
And with his other hand thus o'er his brow
He falls to such perusal of my face
As a would draw it. Long stayed he so;
At last, a little shaking of mine arm,   90
And thrice his head thus waving up and down,
He raised a sigh so piteous and profound
As it did seem to shatter all his bulk,
And end his being. That done, he lets me go,
And with his head over his shoulder turned   95
He seemed to find his way without his eyes,
For out-a-doors he went without their helps
And to the last bended their light on me.

POLONIUS Come, go with me, I will go seek the king.
This is the very ecstasy of love,   100
Whose violent property fordoes itself,
And leads the will to desperate undertakings
As oft as any passion under heaven
That does afflict our natures. I am sorry.
What, have you given him any hard words of late?   105

OPHELIA No my good lord; but as you did command,
I did repel his letters, and denied
His access to me.

POLONIUS   That hath made him mad.
I am sorry that with better heed and judgement
I had not quoted him. I feared he did but trifle,   110
And meant to wrack thee, but beshrew my jealousy.
By heaven, it is as proper to our age
To cast beyond ourselves in our opinions

As it is common for the younger sort
To lack discretion. Come, go we to the king.   115
This must be known, which being kept close, might move
More grief to hide than hate to utter love.
Come.

                                                        Exeunt

2.2 *Flourish. Enter* KING *and* QUEEN, ROSENCRANTZ *and* GUILDENSTERN,
with others

CLAUDIUS Welcome dear Rosencrantz and Guildenstern!
          Moreover that we much did long to see you,
          The need we have to use you did provoke
          Our hasty sending. Something have you heard
          Of Hamlet's transformation – so call it,   5
          Sith nor th'exterior nor the inward man
          Resembles that it was. What it should be,
          More than his father's death, that thus hath put him
          So much from th'understanding of himself,
          I cannot dream of. I entreat you both,   10
          That being of so young days brought up with him,
          And sith so neighboured to his youth and haviour,
          That you vouchsafe your rest here in our court
          Some little time, so by your companies
          To draw him on to pleasures, and to gather   15
          So much as from occasion you may glean,
          Whether aught to us unknown afflicts him thus,
          That opened lies within our remedy.
GERTRUDE Good gentlemen, he hath much talked of you,
          And sure I am, two men there is not living   20
          To whom he more adheres. If it will please you
          To show us so much gentry and good will
          As to expend your time with us a while,
          For the supply and profit of our hope,
          Your visitation shall receive such thanks   25
          As fits a king's remembrance.
ROSENCRANTZ   Both your majesties
          Might by the sovereign power you have of us
          Put your dread pleasures more into command
          Than to entreaty.

GUILDENSTERN   But we both obey,
          And here give up ourselves in the full bent   30
          To lay our service freely at your feet
          To be commanded.
CLAUDIUS Thanks Rosencrantz, and gentle Guildenstern.
GERTRUDE Thanks Guildenstern, and gentle Rosencrantz.
          And I beseech you instantly to visit   35
          My too much changèd son. Go some of you
          And bring these gentlemen where Hamlet is.
GUILDENSTERN Heavens make our presence and our practices
          Pleasant and helpful to him.
GERTRUDE   Ay, amen.
    Exeunt Rosencrantz and Guildenstern [and some Attendants]

Enter POLONIUS

POLONIUS Th'ambassadors from Norway, my good lord,   40
          Are joyfully returned.
CLAUDIUS Thou still hast been the father of good news.
POLONIUS Have I my lord? Assure you, my good liege,
          I hold my duty, as I hold my soul,
          Both to my God and to my gracious king;   45
          And I do think, or else this brain of mine
          Hunts not the trail of policy so sure
          As it hath used to do, that I have found
          The very cause of Hamlet's lunacy.
CLAUDIUS Oh speak of that, that do I long to hear.   50
POLONIUS Give first admittance to th'ambassadors;
          My news shall be the fruit to that great feast.
CLAUDIUS Thyself do grace to them and bring them in.
                    [Exit Polonius]
          He tells me, my dear Gertrude, he hath found
          The head and source of all your son's distemper.   55
GERTRUDE I doubt it is no other but the main:
          His father's death, and our o'erhasty marriage.
CLAUDIUS Well, we shall sift him.

Enter POLONIUS, VOLTEMAND *and* CORNELIUS

          Welcome my good friends.
    Say Voltemand, what from our brother Norway?

VOLTEMAND Most fair return of greetings and desires.   60
        Upon our first, he sent out to suppress
        His nephew's levies, which to him appeared
        To be a preparation 'gainst the Polack;
        But better looked into, he truly found
        It was against your highness; whereat grieved   65
        That so his sickness, age and impotence
        Was falsely borne in hand, sends out arrests
        On Fortinbras, which he in brief obeys,
        Receives rebuke from Norway, and in fine
        Makes vow before his uncle never more   70
        To give th'assay of arms against your majesty.
        Whereon old Norway, overcome with joy,
        Gives him three thousand crowns in annual fee,
        And his commission to employ those soldiers,
        So levied as before, against the Polack;   75
        With an entreaty, herein further shown,
        That it might please you to give quiet pass
        Through your dominions for this enterprise,
        On such regards of safety and allowance
        As therein are set down.
                [*Gives a document*]
CLAUDIUS   It likes us well,   80
        And at our more considered time we'll read,
        Answer, and think upon this business.
        Meantime, we thank you for your well-took labour.
        Go to your rest; at night we'll feast together.
        Most welcome home.
                    Exeunt Ambassadors
POLONIUS   This business is well ended.   85
        My liege, and madam, to expostulate
        What majesty should be, what duty is,
        Why day is day, night night, and time is time,
        Were nothing but to waste night, day, and time.
        Therefore, since brevity is the soul of wit   90
        And tediousness the limbs and outward flourishes,
        I will be brief. Your noble son is mad.
        Mad call I it, for to define true madness,
        What is't but to be nothing else but mad?
        But let that go.
GERTRUDE   More matter with less art.   95

POLONIUS Madam, I swear I use no art at all.
        That he is mad, 'tis true; 'tis true 'tis pity,
        And pity 'tis 'tis true – a foolish figure,
        But farewell it, for I will use no art.
        Mad let us grant him then, and now remains   100
        That we find out the cause of this effect,
        Or rather say, the cause of this defect,
        For this effect defective comes by cause.
        Thus it remains, and the remainder thus.
        Perpend.   105
        I have a daughter – have while she is mine –
        Who in her duty and obedience, mark,
        Hath given me this. Now gather and surmise.
                    Reads the letter
'To the celestial, and my soul's idol, the most beautified Ophelia,' –
That's an ill phrase, a vile phrase, 'beautified' is a vile phrase – but   110
you shall hear. Thus:
'In her excellent white bosom, these, *et cetera*.'
GERTRUDE Came this from Hamlet to her?
POLONIUS Good madam stay awhile, I will be faithful.
        'Doubt thou the stars are fire,   115
        Doubt that the sun doth move,
        Doubt truth to be a liar,
        But never doubt I love.
'O dear Ophelia, I am ill at these numbers, I have not art to reckon
my groans; but that I love thee best, O most best, believe it. Adieu.   120
        'Thine evermore, most dear lady, whilst this machine is
              to him, Hamlet.'
        This in obedience hath my daughter shown me,
        And, more above, hath his solicitings,
        As they fell out, by time, by means, and place,   125
        All given to mine ear.
CLAUDIUS   But how hath she
        Received his love?
POLONIUS   What do you think of me?
CLAUDIUS As of a man faithful and honourable.
POLONIUS I would fain prove so. But what might you think,
        When I had seen this hot love on the wing –   130
        As I perceived it, I must tell you that,
        Before my daughter told me – what might you,
        Or my dear majesty your queen here, think,

If I had played the desk, or table-book,
Or given my heart a winking, mute and dumb,   135
Or looked upon this love with idle sight –
What might you think? No, I went round to work,
And my young mistress thus I did bespeak:
'Lord Hamlet is a prince out of thy star.
This must not be.' And then I prescripts gave her,   140
That she should lock herself from his resort,
Admit no messengers, receive no tokens.
Which done, she took the fruits of my advice,
And he, repulsed – a short tale to make –
Fell into a sadness, then into a fast,   145
Thence to a watch, thence into a weakness,
Thence to a lightness, and by this declension
Into the madness wherein now he raves,
And all we mourn for.

CLAUDIUS   Do you think 'tis this?
GERTRUDE It may be, very like.   150
POLONIUS Hath there been such a time, I'ld fain know that,
That I have positively said, 'tis so,
When it proved otherwise?
CLAUDIUS   Not that I know.
POLONIUS Take this from this, if this be otherwise.
If circumstances lead me, I will find   155
Where truth is hid, though it were hid indeed
Within the centre.
CLAUDIUS   How may we try it further?
POLONIUS You know sometimes he walks four hours together
Here in the lobby.
GERTRUDE   So he does indeed.
POLONIUS At such a time I'll loose my daughter to him.   160
Be you and I behind an arras then.
Mark the encounter: if he love her not,
And be not from his reason fallen thereon,
Let me be no assistant for a state,
But keep a farm and carters.
CLAUDIUS   We will try it.   165

Enter HAMLET *reading on a book*

GERTRUDE But look where sadly the poor wretch comes reading.
POLONIUS Away, I do beseech you both, away.

      I'll board him presently.

        Exeunt Claudius and Gertrude [and Attendants]

                Oh give me leave.

      How does my good Lord Hamlet?

HAMLET Well, God-a-mercy.   170

POLONIUS Do you know me, my lord?

HAMLET Excellent well, y'are a fishmonger.

POLONIUS Not I my lord.

HAMLET Then I would you were so honest a man.

POLONIUS Honest my lord?   175

HAMLET Ay sir. To be honest, as this world goes, is to be one man
    picked out of ten thousand.

POLONIUS That's very true my lord.

HAMLET For if the sun breed maggots in a dead dog, being a good
    kissing carrion – Have you a daughter?   180

POLONIUS I have my lord.

HAMLET Let her not walk i'th'sun. Conception is a blessing, but as your
    daughter may conceive – Friend, look to't.

POLONIUS (*Aside*) How say you by that? Still harping on my daughter.
    Yet he knew me not at first, a said I was a fishmonger – a is far   185
    gone, far gone. And truly, in my youth I suffered much extremity
    for love, very near this. I'll speak to him again. – What do you read
    my lord?

HAMLET Words, words, words.

POLONIUS What is the matter, my lord?   190

HAMLET Between who?

POLONIUS I mean the matter that you read, my lord.

HAMLET Slanders sir, for the satirical rogue says here that old men have
    grey beards, that their faces are wrinkled, their eyes purging thick
    amber and plumtree gum, and that they have a plentiful lack of wit,   195
    together with most weak hams. All which sir, though I most
    powerfully and potently believe, yet I hold it not honesty to have
    it thus set down. For yourself sir shall grow old as I am, if like a
    crab you could go backward.

POLONIUS (*Aside*) Though this be madness, yet there is method   200
    in't. – Will you walk out of the air, my lord?

HAMLET Into my grave?

POLONIUS Indeed that's out of the air. (*Aside*) How pregnant sometimes
    his replies are! a happiness that often madness hits on, which reason
    and sanity could not so prosperously be delivered of. I will leave   205
    him, and suddenly contrive the means of meeting between him and

my daughter. – My honourable lord, I will most humbly take my
leave of you.

HAMLET You cannot sir take from me anything that I will more
willingly part withal; except my life, except my life, except my life. 210

POLONIUS Fare you well my lord.

HAMLET These tedious old fools!

Enter GUILDENSTERN *and* ROSENCRANTZ

POLONIUS You go to seek the Lord Hamlet, there he is.

ROSENCRANTZ God save you sir.

[*Exit Polonius*]

GUILDENSTERN My honoured lord!   215

ROSENCRANTZ My most dear lord!

HAMLET My excellent good friends! How dost thou Guildenstern? Ah,
Rosencrantz. Good lads, how do you both?

ROSENCRANTZ As the indifferent children of the earth.

GUILDENSTERN Happy in that we are not over-happy; on Fortune's   220
cap we are not the very button.

HAMLET Nor the soles of her shoe?

ROSENCRANTZ Neither, my lord.

HAMLET Then you live about her waist, or in the middle of her favours?

GUILDENSTERN Faith, her privates we.   225

HAMLET In the secret parts of Fortune? Oh most true, she is a
strumpet. What news?

ROSENCRANTZ None my lord, but that the world's grown honest.

HAMLET Then is doomsday near – but your news is not true. Let me
question more in particular. What have you, my good friends,   230
deserved at the hands of Fortune, that she sends you to prison
hither?

GUILDENSTERN Prison, my lord?

HAMLET Denmark's a prison.

ROSENCRANTZ Then is the world one.   235

HAMLET A goodly one, in which there are many confines, wards, and
dungeons; Denmark being one o'th'worst.

ROSENCRANTZ We think not so my lord.

HAMLET Why then 'tis none to you, for there is nothing either good
or bad but thinking makes it so. To me it is a prison.   240

ROSENCRANTZ Why then your ambition makes it one; 'tis too narrow
for your mind.

HAMLET O God, I could be bounded in a nutshell, and count myself
a king of infinite space, were it not that I have bad dreams.

GUILDENSTERN Which dreams indeed are ambition, for the very   245
  substance of the ambitious is merely the shadow of a dream.

HAMLET A dream itself is but a shadow.

ROSENCRANTZ Truly, and I hold ambition of so airy and light a quality
  that it is but a shadow's shadow.

HAMLET Then are our beggars bodies, and our monarchs and out-   250
  stretched heroes the beggars' shadows. Shall we to th'court? for by
  my fay I cannot reason.

BOTH We'll wait upon you.

HAMLET No such matter. I will not sort you with the rest of my
  servants; for to speak to you like an honest man, I am most   255
  dreadfully attended. But in the beaten way of friendship, what make
  you at Elsinore?

ROSENCRANTZ To visit you my lord, no other occasion.

HAMLET Beggar that I am, I am even poor in thanks, but I thank
  you – and sure, dear friends, my thanks are too dear a halfpenny.   260
  Were you not sent for? Is it your own inclining? Is it a free
  visitation? Come, deal justly with me. Come, come. Nay, speak.

GUILDENSTERN What should we say my lord?

HAMLET Why, anything but to the purpose. You were sent for – and
  there is a kind of confession in your looks which your modesties   265
  have not craft enough to colour. I know the good king and queen
  have sent for you.

ROSENCRANTZ To what end my lord?

HAMLET That you must teach me. But let me conjure you, by the rights
  of our fellowship, by the consonancy of our youth, by the obligation   270
  of our ever-preserved love, and by what more dear a better proposer
  can charge you withal, be even and direct with me, whether you
  were sent for or no.

ROSENCRANTZ (*To Guildenstern*) What say you?

HAMLET (*Aside*) Nay then I have an eye of you. – If you love me, hold   275
  not off.

GUILDENSTERN My lord, we were sent for.

HAMLET I will tell you why. So shall my anticipation prevent your
  discovery, and your secrecy to the king and queen moult no feather.
  I have of late, but wherefore I know not, lost all my mirth, forgone   280
  all custom of exercises; and indeed it goes so heavily with my
  disposition that this goodly frame, the earth, seems to me a sterile
  promontory; this most excellent canopy the air, look you, this brave
  o'erhanging firmament, this majestical roof fretted with golden
  fire – why, it appeareth no other thing to me but a foul and pestilent   285

congregation of vapours. What a piece of work is a man! How noble
in reason, how infinite in faculties, in form and moving how express
and admirable, in action how like an angel, in apprehension how
like a god! The beauty of the world, the paragon of animals – and
yet to me, what is this quintessence of dust? Man delights not   290
me – no, nor woman neither, though by your smiling you seem to
say so.

ROSENCRANTZ My lord, there was no such stuff in my thoughts.

HAMLET Why did ye laugh then, when I said man delights not me?

ROSENCRANTZ To think, my lord, if you delight not in man, what   295
lenten entertainment the players shall receive from you. We coted
them on the way, and hither are they coming to offer you service.

HAMLET He that plays the king shall be welcome, his majesty shall have
tribute of me; the adventurous knight shall use his foil and target,
the lover shall not sigh gratis, the humorous man shall end his part   300
in peace, the clown shall make those laugh whose lungs are tickle
o'th'sere, and the lady shall say her mind freely – or the blank verse
shall halt for't. What players are they?

ROSENCRANTZ Even those you were wont to take such delight in, the
tragedians of the city.   305

HAMLET How chances it they travel? their residence, both in reputation
and profit, was better both ways.

ROSENCRANTZ I think their inhibition comes by the means of the late
innovation.

HAMLET Do they hold the same estimation they did when I was in the   310
city? Are they so followed?

ROSENCRANTZ No indeed are they not.

HAMLET How comes it? Do they grow rusty?

ROSENCRANTZ Nay, their endeavour keeps in the wonted pace, but
there is sir an eyrie of children, little eyases, that cry out on the   315
top of question and are most tyrannically clapped for't. These are
now the fashion, and so be-rattle the common stages (so they call
them) that many wearing rapiers are afraid of goose-quills, and dare
scarce come thither.

HAMLET What, are they children? Who maintains 'em? How are they   320
escoted? Will they pursue the quality no longer than they can sing?
Will they not say afterwards, if they should grow themselves to
common players – as it is most like if their means are no better, their
writers do them wrong to make them exclaim against their own
succession?   325

ROSENCRANTZ Faith, there has been much to do on both sides, and

the nation holds it no sin to tar them to controversy. There was
for a while no money bid for argument unless the poet and the player
went to cuffs in the question.

HAMLET Is't possible? 330

GUILDENSTERN Oh there has been much throwing about of brains.

HAMLET Do the boys carry it away?

ROSENCRANTZ Ay that they do my lord, Hercules and his load too.

HAMLET It is not very strange, for my uncle is king of Denmark, and
those that would make mouths at him while my father lived give 335
twenty, forty, fifty, a hundred ducats apiece for his picture in little.
'Sblood, there is something in this more than natural, if philosophy
could find it out.

A flourish

GUILDENSTERN There are the players.

HAMLET Gentlemen, you are welcome to Elsinore. Your hands, come 340
then. Th'appurtenance of welcome is fashion and ceremony. Let
me comply with you in this garb, lest my extent to the players, which
I tell you must show fairly outwards, should more appear like
entertainment than yours. You are welcome – but my uncle-father
and aunt-mother are deceived. 345

GUILDENSTERN In what my dear lord?

HAMLET I am but mad north-north-west. When the wind is southerly,
I know a hawk from a handsaw.

Enter POLONIUS

POLONIUS Well be with you gentlemen.

HAMLET Hark you Guildenstern, and you too – at each ear a hearer. 350
That great baby you see there is not yet out of his swaddling clouts.

ROSENCRANTZ Happily he's the second time come to them, for they
say an old man is twice a child.

HAMLET I will prophesy: he comes to tell me of the players, mark
it. – You say right sir, a Monday morning, 'twas then indeed. 355

POLONIUS My lord, I have news to tell you.

HAMLET My lord, I have news to tell you. When Roscius was an actor
in Rome –

POLONIUS The actors are come hither my lord.

HAMLET Buzz, buzz! 360

POLONIUS Upon my honour.

HAMLET Then came each actor on his ass –

POLONIUS The best actors in the world, either for tragedy, comedy,
history, pastoral, pastoral-comical, historical-pastoral, tragical-

historical, tragical-comical-historical-pastoral, scene individable or   365
poem unlimited. Seneca cannot be too heavy, nor Plautus too light.
For the law of writ and the liberty, these are the only men.

HAMLET O Jephtha judge of Israel, what a treasure hadst thou!

POLONIUS What a treasure had he my lord?

HAMLET Why –   370

> 'One fair daughter and no more,
> The which he lovèd passing well.'

POLONIUS Still on my daughter.

HAMLET Am I not i'th'right, old Jephtha?

POLONIUS If you call me Jephtha my lord, I have a daughter that I   375
love passing well.

HAMLET Nay, that follows not.

POLONIUS What follows then my lord?

HAMLET Why –

> 'As by lot God wot,'   380

And then you know –

> 'It came to pass, as most like it was,' –

the first row of the pious chanson will show you more, for look where
my abridgement comes.

Enter the PLAYERS

Y'are welcome masters, welcome all. I am glad to see thee well.   385
Welcome good friends. Oh, my old friend! why, thy face is valanced
since I saw thee last; com'st thou to beard me in Denmark? What,
my young lady and mistress – byrlady, your ladyship is nearer to
heaven than when I saw you last by the altitude of a chopine. Pray
God your voice like a piece of uncurrent gold be not cracked within   390
the ring. Masters, you are all welcome. We'll e'en to't like French
falconers, fly at anything we see: we'll have a speech straight. Come
give us a taste of your quality: come, a passionate speech.

I PLAYER What speech, my good lord?

HAMLET I heard thee speak me a speech once, but it was never acted,   395
or if it was, not above once, for the play I remember pleased not
the million: 'twas caviary to the general. But it was, as I received
it, and others whose judgements in such matters cried in the top
of mine, an excellent play, well digested in the scenes, set down with
as much modesty as cunning. I remember one said there were no   400
sallets in the lines to make the matter savoury, nor no matter in
the phrase that might indict the author of affectation, but called it
an honest method, as wholesome as sweet and by very much more

handsome than fine. One speech in't I chiefly loved, 'twas Aeneas'
tale to Dido, and thereabout of it especially where he speaks of   405
Priam's slaughter. If it live in your memory, begin at this line, let
me see, let me see –

    'The rugged Pyrrhus, like th'Hyrcanian beast' –
'Tis not so, it begins with Pyrrhus –

      'The rugged Pyrrhus, he whose sable arms,   410
      Black as his purpose, did the night resemble
      When he lay couchèd in the ominous horse,
      Hath now this dread and black complexion smeared
      With heraldy more dismal. Head to foot
      Now is he total gules, horridly tricked   415
      With blood of fathers, mothers, daughters, sons,
      Baked and impasted with the parching streets,
      That lend a tyrannous and a damnèd light
      To their lord's murder. Roasted in wrath and fire,
      And thus o'er-sizèd with coagulate gore,   420
      With eyes like carbuncles, the hellish Pyrrhus
      Old grandsire Priam seeks –'
So, proceed you.
POLONIUS 'Fore God my lord, well spoken, with good accent and good
    discretion.   425
I PLAYER   'Anon he finds him,
      Striking too short at Greeks; his antique sword,
      Rebellious to his arm, lies where it falls,
      Repugnant to command. Unequal matched,
      Pyrrhus at Priam drives, in rage strikes wide,   430
      But with the whiff and wind of his fell sword
      Th'unnervèd father falls. Then senseless Ilium,
      Seeming to feel this blow, with flaming top
      Stoops to his base, and with a hideous crash
      Takes prisoner Pyrrhus' ear; for lo, his sword,   435
      Which was declining on the milky head
      Of reverend Priam, seemed i'th'air to stick.
      So, as a painted tyrant, Pyrrhus stood,
      And like a neutral to his will and matter,
      Did nothing.   440
      But as we often see against some storm,
      A silence in the heavens, the rack stand still,
      The bold winds speechless, and the orb below
      As hush as death, anon the dreadful thunder

Doth rend the region; so after Pyrrhus' pause,   445
A rousèd vengeance sets him new a-work,
And never did the Cyclops' hammers fall
On Mars's armour, forged for proof eterne,
With less remorse than Pyrrhus' bleeding sword
Now falls on Priam.   450
Out, out, thou strumpet Fortune! All you gods,
In general synod take away her power,
Break all the spokes and fellies from her wheel,
And bowl the round nave down the hill of heaven
As low as to the fiends.'   455

POLONIUS This is too long.

HAMLET It shall to th' barber's with your beard. Prithee say on.
He's for a jig or a tale of bawdry, or he sleeps. Say on, come to
Hecuba.

I PLAYER 'But who – ah woe! – had seen the mobled queen –'   460

HAMLET The mobled queen?

POLONIUS That's good, 'mobled queen' is good.

I PLAYER 'Run barefoot up and down, threat'ning the flames
With bisson rheum, a clout upon that head
Where late the diadem stood, and, for a robe,   465
About her lank and all o'er-teemèd loins
A blanket, in th'alarm of fear caught up –
Who this had seen, with tongue in venom steeped
'Gainst Fortune's state would treason have pronounced.
But if the gods themselves did see her then,   470
When she saw Pyrrhus make malicious sport
In mincing with his sword her husband's limbs,
The instant burst of clamour that she made,
Unless things mortal move them not at all,
Would have made milch the burning eyes of heaven,
And passion in the gods.   475

POLONIUS Look where he has not turned his colour, and has tears in's
eyes. Prithee no more.

HAMLET 'Tis well, I'll have thee speak out the rest of this soon. – Good
my lord, will you see the players well bestowed? Do you hear, let 480
them be well used, for they are the abstract and brief chronicles
of the time. After your death you were better have a bad epitaph
than their ill report while you live.

POLONIUS My lord, I will use them according to their desert.

HAMLET God's bodkin man, much better. Use every man after his   485

desert, and who shall scape whipping? Use them after your own
honour and dignity; the less they deserve, the more merit is in your
bounty. Take them in.

POLONIUS Come sirs.   *Exit Polonius*

HAMLET Follow him friends, we'll hear a play tomorrow. – Dost thou   490
hear me old friend, can you play *The Murder of Gonzago?*

I PLAYER Ay my lord.

HAMLET We'll ha't tomorrow night. You could for a need study a
speech of some dozen or sixteen lines, which I would set down and
insert in't, could you not?   495

I PLAYER Ay my lord.

HAMLET Very well. Follow that lord, and look you mock him not.

Exeunt Players

My good friends, I'll leave you till night. You are welcome to
Elsinore.

ROSENCRANTZ Good my lord.   500

Exeunt Rosencrantz and Guildenstern

HAMLET Ay so, God bye to you. Now I am alone.
O what a rogue and peasant slave am I!
Is it not monstrous that this player here,
But in a fiction, in a dream of passion,
Could force his soul so to his own conceit   505
That from her working all his visage wanned,
Tears in his eyes, distraction in's aspect,
A broken voice, and his whole function suiting
With forms to his conceit? And all for nothing?
For Hecuba!   510
What's Hecuba to him, or he to Hecuba,
That he should weep for her? What would he do,
Had he the motive and the cue for passion
That I have? He would drown the stage with tears,
And cleave the general ear with horrid speech,   515
Make mad the guilty and appal the free,
Confound the ignorant, and amaze indeed
The very faculties of eyes and ears. Yet I,
A dull and muddy-mettled rascal, peak
Like John-a-dreams, unpregnant of my cause,   520
And can say nothing – no, not for a king,
Upon whose property and most dear life
A damned defeat was made. Am I a coward?
Who calls me villain, breaks my pate across,

Plucks off my beard and blows it in my face,   525
Tweaks me by th'nose, gives me the lie i'th'throat
As deep as to the lungs? Who does me this?
Ha, 'swounds, I should take it, for it cannot be
But I am pigeon-livered, and lack gall
To make oppression bitter, or ere this   530
I should ha' fatted all the region kites
With this slave's offal. Bloody, bawdy villain!
Remorseless, treacherous, lecherous, kindless villain!
Oh, vengeance!
Why, what an ass am I! This is most brave,   535
That I, the son of the dear murderèd,
Prompted to my revenge by heaven and hell,
Must like a whore unpack my heart with words,
And fall a-cursing like a very drab,
A scullion!   540
Fie upon't, foh! About, my brains. Hum, I have heard
That guilty creatures sitting at a play
Have by the very cunning of the scene
Been struck so to the soul, that presently
They have proclaimed their malefactions;   545
For murder, though it have no tongue, will speak
With most miraculous organ. I'll have these players
Play something like the murder of my father
Before mine uncle. I'll observe his looks,
I'll tent him to the quick. If a do blench,   550
I know my course. The spirit that I have seen
May be a devil – and the devil hath power
T'assume a pleasing shape. Yea, and perhaps,
Out of my weakness and my melancholy,
As he is very potent with such spirits,   555
Abuses me to damn me. I'll have grounds
More relative than this. The play's the thing
Wherein I'll catch the conscience of the king.   *Exit*

3.1 *Enter* KING, QUEEN, POLONIUS, OPHELIA, ROSENCRANTZ, GUILDEN-
STERN, LORDS

CLAUDIUS And can you by no drift of circumstance
            Get from him why he puts on this confusion,

           Grating so harshly all his days of quiet
           With turbulent and dangerous lunacy?
ROSENCRANTZ He does confess he feels himself distracted,   5
           But from what cause a will by no means speak.
GUILDENSTERN Nor do we find him forward to be sounded,
           But with a crafty madness keeps aloof
           When we would bring him on to some confession
           Of his true state.
GERTRUDE   Did he receive you well?   10
ROSENCRANTZ Most like a gentleman.
GUILDENSTERN But with much forcing of his disposition.
ROSENCRANTZ Niggard of question, but of our demands
           Most free in his reply.
GERTRUDE   Did you assay him
           To any pastime?   15
ROSENCRANTZ Madam, it so fell out that certain players
           We o'er-raught on the way; of these we told him,
           And there did seem in him a kind of joy
           To hear of it. They are about the court,
           And as I think, they have already order   20
           This night to play before him.
POLONIUS   'Tis most true,
           And he beseeched me to entreat your majesties
           To hear and see the matter.
CLAUDIUS With all my heart, and it doth much content me
           To hear him so inclined.   25
           Good gentlemen, give him a further edge,
           And drive his purpose on to these delights.
ROSENCRANTZ We shall my lord.
                Exeunt Rosencrantz and Guildenstern
CLAUDIUS   Sweet Gertrude, leave us too,
           For we have closely sent for Hamlet hither,
           That he, as 'twere by accident, may here   30
           Affront Ophelia. Her father and myself,
           Lawful espials,
           Will so bestow ourselves, that seeing unseen,
           We may of their encounter frankly judge,
           And gather by him, as he is behaved,   35
           If't be th'affliction of his love or no
           That thus he suffers for.
GERTRUDE   I shall obey you.

And for your part Ophelia, I do wish
That your good beauties be the happy cause
Of Hamlet's wildness. So shall I hope your virtues   40
Will bring him to his wonted way again,
To both your honours.

OPHELIA   Madam, I wish it may.

[*Exit Gertrude with Lords*]

POLONIUS Ophelia walk you here. – Gracious, so please you,
We will bestow ourselves. – Read on this book,
That show of such an exercise may colour   45
Your loneliness. – We are oft to blame in this:
'Tis too much proved, that with devotion's visage,
And pious action, we do sugar o'er
The devil himself.

CLAUDIUS (*Aside*)   Oh, 'tis too true.
How smart a lash that speech doth give my conscience!   50
The harlot's cheek, beautied with plastering art,
Is not more ugly to the thing that helps it
Than is my deed to my most painted word.
O heavy burden!

POLONIUS I hear him coming. Let's withdraw, my lord.   55

Exeunt Claudius and Polonius

Enter HAMLET

HAMLET To be, or not to be, that is the question –
Whether 'tis nobler in the mind to suffer
The slings and arrows of outrageous fortune,
Or to take arms against a sea of troubles,
And by opposing end them. To die, to sleep –   60
No more; and by a sleep to say we end
The heart-ache and the thousand natural shocks
That flesh is heir to – 'tis a consummation
Devoutly to be wished. To die, to sleep –
To sleep, perchance to dream. Ay, there's the rub,   65
For in that sleep of death what dreams may come,
When we have shuffled off this mortal coil,
Must give us pause. There's the respect
That makes calamity of so long life,
For who would bear the whips and scorns of time,   70
Th'oppressor's wrong, the proud man's contumely,
The pangs of disprized love, the law's delay,

The insolence of office, and the spurns
That patient merit of th'unworthy takes,
When he himself might his quietus make   75
With a bare bodkin? Who would fardels bear,
To grunt and sweat under a weary life,
But that the dread of something after death,
The undiscovered country from whose bourn
No traveller returns, puzzles the will,   80
And makes us rather bear those ills we have
Then fly to others that we know not of?
Thus conscience does make cowards of us all,
And thus the native hue of resolution
Is sicklied o'er with the pale cast of thought,   85
And enterprises of great pitch and moment
With this regard their currents turn awry
And lose the name of action. Soft you now,
The fair Ophelia. – Nymph, in thy orisons
Be all my sins remembered.

OPHELIA   Good my lord,   90
How does your honour for this many a day?

HAMLET I humbly thank you, well, well, well.

OPHELIA My lord, I have remembrances of yours
That I have longèd long to re-deliver.
I pray you now receive them.

HAMLET   No, not I,   95
I never gave you aught.

OPHELIA My honoured lord, you know right well you did,
And with them words of so sweet breath composed
As made the things more rich. Their perfume lost,
Take these again, for to the noble mind   100
Rich gifts wax poor when givers prove unkind.
There my lord.

HAMLET Ha, ha, are you honest?

OPHELIA My lord?

HAMLET Are you fair?   105

OPHELIA What means your lordship?

HAMLET That if you be honest and fair, your honesty should admit no
   discourse to your beauty.

OPHELIA Could beauty, my lord, have better commerce than with
   honesty?   110

HAMLET Ay truly, for the power of beauty will sooner transform

honesty from what it is to a bawd, than the force of honesty can
translate beauty into his likeness. This was sometime a paradox, but
now the time gives it proof. I did love you once.

OPHELIA Indeed my lord you made me believe so.   115

HAMLET You should not have believed me, for virtue cannot so
inoculate our old stock but we shall relish of it. I loved you not.

OPHELIA I was the more deceived.

HAMLET Get thee to a nunnery – why wouldst thou be a breeder of
sinners? I am myself indifferent honest, but yet I could accuse me   120
of such things, that it were better my mother had not borne me.
I am very proud, revengeful, ambitious, with more offences at my
beck than I have thoughts to put them in, imagination to give them
shape, or time to act them in. What should such fellows as I do
crawling between earth and heaven? We are arrant knaves all,   125
believe none of us. Go thy ways to a nunnery. Where's your father?

OPHELIA At home my lord.

HAMLET Let the doors be shut upon him, that he may play the fool
nowhere but in's own house. Farewell.

OPHELIA Oh help him you sweet heavens!   130

HAMLET If thou dost marry, I'll give thee this plague for thy dowry:
be thou as chaste as ice, as pure as snow, thou shalt not escape
calumny. Get thee to a nunnery, go. Farewell. Or if thou wilt needs
marry, marry a fool, for wise men know well enough what monsters
you make of them. To a nunnery go, and quickly too. Farewell.   135

OPHELIA O heavenly powers, restore him!

HAMLET I have heard of your paintings too, well enough. God hath
given you one face and you make yourselves another. You jig, you
amble, and you lisp, you nickname God's creatures, and make your
wantonness your ignorance. Go to, I'll no more on't, it hath made   140
me mad. I say we will have no mo marriages. Those that are married
already, all but one shall live, the rest shall keep as they are. To
a nunnery, go.   *Exit*

OPHELIA Oh what a noble mind is here o'erthrown!
        The courtier's, soldier's, scholar's, eye, tongue, sword,   145
        Th'expectancy and rose of the fair state,
        The glass of fashion and the mould of form,
        Th'observed of all observers, quite, quite down,
        And I of ladies most deject and wretched,
        That sucked the honey of his music vows,   150
        Now see that noble and most sovereign reason,
        Like sweet bells jangled, out of time and harsh;

That unmatched form and feature of blown youth
Blasted with ecstasy. Oh woe is me
T'have seen what I have seen, see what I see.   155

Enter KING *and* POLONIUS

CLAUDIUS Love? His affections do not that way tend;
         Nor what he spake, though it lacked form a little,
         Was not like madness. There's something in his soul
         O'er which his melancholy sits on brood,
         And I do doubt the hatch and the disclose   160
         Will be some danger; which for to prevent,
         I have in quick determination
         Thus set it down: he shall with speed to England
         For the demand of our neglected tribute.
         Haply the seas, and countries different,   165
         With variable objects, shall expel
         This something-settled matter in his heart,
         Whereon his brains still beating puts him thus
         From fashion of himself. What think you on't?
POLONIUS It shall do well. But yet do I believe   170
         The origin and commencement of his grief
         Sprung from neglected love. How now Ophelia?
         You need not tell us what Lord Hamlet said,
         We heard it all. My lord, do as you please,
         But if you hold it fit, after the play,   175
         Let his queen mother all alone entreat him
         To show his grief. Let her be round with him,
         And I'll be placed, so please you, in the ear
         Of all their conference. If she find him not,
         To England send him; or confine him where   180
         Your wisdom best shall think.
CLAUDIUS   It shall be so.
         Madness in great ones must not unwatched go.

                                                    Exeunt

[3.2] *Enter* HAMLET *and two or three of the* PLAYERS

HAMLET Speak the speech I pray you as I pronounced it to you,
       trippingly on the tongue; but if you mouth it as many of our players
       do, I had as lief the town-crier spoke my lines. Nor do not saw the

air too much with your hand thus, but use all gently; for in the
very torrent, tempest, and, as I may say, whirlwind of your passion,   5
you must acquire and beget a temperance that may give it
smoothness. Oh, it offends me to the soul to hear a robustious
periwig-pated fellow tear a passion to totters, to very rags, to split
the ears of the groundlings, who for the most part are capable of
nothing but inexplicable dumb-shows and noise. I would have such   10
a fellow whipped for o'erdoing Termagant – it out-Herods Herod.
Pray you avoid it.

I PLAYER I warrant your honour.

HAMLET Be not too tame neither, but let your own discretion be your
tutor. Suit the action to the word, the word to the action, with this   15
special observance, that you o'erstep not the modesty of nature. For
anything so o'erdone is from the purpose of playing, whose end both
at the first and now, was and is, to hold as 'twere the mirror up
to nature; to show virtue her own feature, scorn her own image,
and the very age and body of the time his form and pressure. Now   20
this overdone, or come tardy off, though it makes the unskilful
laugh, cannot but make the judicious grieve, the censure of the
which one must in your allowance o'erweigh a whole theatre of
others. Oh, there be players that I have seen play, and heard others
praise and that highly, not to speak it profanely, that neither having   25
th'accent of Christians, nor the gait of Christian, pagan, nor man,
have so strutted and bellowed that I have thought some of nature's
journeymen had made men, and not made them well, they imitated
humanity so abominably.

I PLAYER I hope we have reformed that indifferently with us, sir.   30

HAMLET Oh reform it altogether. And let those that play your clowns
speak no more than is set down for them, for there be of them that
will themselves laugh, to set on some quantity of barren spectators
to laugh too, though in the meantime some necessary question of
the play be then to be considered. That's villainous, and shows   35
a most pitiful ambition in the fool that uses it. Go make you ready.

Exeunt Players

Enter POLONIUS, ROSENCRANTZ *and* GUILDENSTERN

How now my lord, will the king hear this piece of work?

POLONIUS And the queen too, and that presently.

HAMLET Bid the players make haste.

Exit Polonius

Will you two help to hasten them?   40

ROSENCRANTZ Ay my lord.

Exeunt Rosencrantz and Guildenstern

HAMLET What ho, Horatio!

Enter HORATIO

HORATIO Here sweet lord, at your service.

HAMLET Horatio, thou art e'en as just a man

    As e'er my conversation coped withal.   45

HORATIO Oh my dear lord.

HAMLET   Nay, do not think I flatter,

    For what advancement may I hope from thee,

    That no revenue hast but thy good spirits

    To feed and clothe thee? Why should the poor be flattered?

    No, let the candied tongue lick absurd pomp   50

    And crook the pregnant hinges of the knee

    Where thrift may follow fawning. Dost thou hear?

    Since my dear soul was mistress of her choice,

    And could of men distinguish her election,

    Sh'ath sealed thee for herself, for thou hast been   55

    As one in suffering all that suffers nothing,

    A man that Fortune's buffets and rewards

    Hast tane with equal thanks. And blest are those

    Whose blood and judgement are so well commeddled

    That they are not a pipe for Fortune's finger   60

    To sound what stop she please. Give me that man

    That is not passion's slave, and I will wear him

    In my heart's core, ay in my heart of heart,

    As I do thee. Something too much of this.

    There is a play tonight before the king: 65

    One scene of it comes near the circumstance

    Which I have told thee of my father's death.

    I prithee when thou seest that act afoot,

    Even with the very comment of thy soul

    Observe my uncle. If his occulted guilt   70

    Do not itself unkennel in one speech,

    It is a damnèd ghost that we have seen,

    And my imaginations are as foul

    As Vulcan's stithy. Give him heedful note,

    For I mine eyes will rivet to his face,   75

    And after we will both our judgements join

    In censure of his seeming.

HORATIO   Well my lord.
   If a steal aught the whilst this play is playing
   And scape detecting, I will pay the theft.
          Sound a flourish
HAMLET They are coming to the play. I must be idle.   80
   Get you a place.

Danish march (trumpets and kettle-drums). Enter KING, QUEEN, POLONIUS,
OPHELIA, ROSENCRANTZ, GUILDENSTERN *and other* LORDS *attendant, with his*
GUARD *carrying torches*

CLAUDIUS How fares our cousin Hamlet?
HAMLET Excellent i'faith, of the chameleon's dish: I eat the air,
   promise-crammed. You cannot feed capons so.
CLAUDIUS I have nothing with this answer Hamlet, these words are not   85
   mine.
HAMLET No, nor mine now. – My lord, you played once i'th'university,
   you say.
POLONIUS That did I my lord, and was accounted a good actor.
HAMLET And what did you enact?   90
POLONIUS I did enact Julius Caesar. I was killed i'th'Capitol. Brutus
   killed me.
HAMLET It was a brute part of him to kill so capital a calf there. – Be
   the players ready?
ROSENCRANTZ Ay my lord, they stay upon your patience.   95
GERTRUDE Come hither my dear Hamlet, sit by me.
HAMLET No good mother, here's metal more attractive.
POLONIUS Oh ho, do you mark that?
HAMLET Lady, shall I lie in your lap?
OPHELIA No my lord.   100
HAMLET I mean, my head upon your lap?
OPHELIA Ay my lord.
HAMLET Do you think I meant country matters?
OPHELIA I think nothing my lord.
HAMLET That's a fair thought to lie between maids' legs.   105
OPHELIA What is, my lord?
HAMLET Nothing.
OPHELIA You are merry my lord.
HAMLET Who, I?
OPHELIA Ay my lord.   110
HAMLET O God, your only jig-maker. What should a man do but be

merry? for look you how cheerfully my mother looks, and my father
died within's two hours.

OPHELIA Nay, 'tis twice two months my lord.

HAMLET So long? Nay then let the devil wear black, for I'll have a suit   115
of sables. O heavens! die two months ago, and not forgotten yet?
Then there's hope a great man's memory may outlive his life half
a year, but byrlady a must build churches then, or else shall a suffer
not thinking on, with the hobby-horse, whose epitaph is, 'For O,
for O, the hobby-horse is forgot.'   120

Hoboys play. The dumb-show enters

Enter a KING *and a* QUEEN, *very lovingly, the Queen embracing him. She
kneels and makes show of protestation unto him. He takes her up, and declines
his head upon her neck. He lies him down upon a bank of flowers. She, seeing
him asleep, leaves him. Anon comes in another man, takes off his crown, kisses
it, pours poison in the sleeper's ears, and leaves him. The Queen returns,
finds the King dead, and makes passionate action. The poisoner, with some
two or three mutes, comes in again, seeming to condole with her. The dead
body is carried away. The poisoner woos the Queen with gifts. She seems
harsh awhile, but in the end accepts his love.*   *Exeunt*

OPHELIA What means this my lord?

HAMLET Marry this is miching mallecho, it means mischief.

OPHELIA Belike this show imports the argument of the play?

Enter PROLOGUE

HAMLET We shall know by this fellow; the players cannot keep counsel,
they'll tell all.   125

OPHELIA Will a tell us what this show meant?

HAMLET Ay, or any show that you'll show him. Be not you ashamed
to show, he'll not shame to tell you what it means.

OPHELIA You are naught, you are naught. I'll mark the play.

PROLOGUE For us and for our tragedy,   130
            Here stooping to your clemency,
            We beg your hearing patiently.

HAMLET Is this a prologue, or the posy of a ring?

OPHELIA 'Tis brief my lord.

HAMLET As woman's love.   135

Enter the PLAYER KING *and* QUEEN

PLAYER KING Full thirty times hath Phoebus' cart gone round
    Neptune's salt wash and Tellus' orbèd ground,
    And thirty dozen moons with borrowed sheen
    About the world have times twelve thirties been,
    Since love our hearts, and Hymen did our hands,   140
    Unite commutual in most sacred bands.
PLAYER QUEEN So many journeys may the sun and moon
    Make us again count o'er ere love be done.
    But woe is me, you are so sick of late,
    So far from cheer and from your former state,   145
    That I distrust you. Yet though I distrust,
    Discomfort you my lord it nothing must.
    For women's fear and love hold quantity,
    In neither aught, or in extremity.
    Now what my love is, proof hath made you know;   150
    And as my love is sized, my fear is so.
    [Where love is great, the littlest doubts are fear;
    Where little fears grow great, great love grows there.]
PLAYER KING Faith, I must leave thee love, and shortly too:
    My operant powers their functions leave to do;   155
    And thou shalt live in this fair world behind,
    Honoured, beloved; and haply one as kind
    For husband shalt thou –
PLAYER QUEEN   Oh confound the rest!
    Such love must needs be treason in my breast.
    In second husband let me be accurst: 160
    None wed the second but who killed the first.

HAMLET That's wormwood, wormwood.

PLAYER QUEEN The instances that second marriage move
    Are base respects of thrift, but none of love.
    A second time I kill my husband dead   165
    When second husband kisses me in bed.
PLAYER KING I do believe you think what now you speak,
    But what we do determine oft we break.
    Purpose is but the slave to memory,
    Of violent birth but poor validity,   170
    Which now like fruit unripe sticks on the tree,
    But fall unshaken when they mellow be.
    Most necessary 'tis that we forget

To pay ourselves what to ourselves is debt.
What to ourselves in passion we propose,   175
The passion ending, doth the purpose lose.
The violence of either grief or joy
Their own enactures with themselves destroy.
Where joy most revels, grief doth most lament;
Grief joys, joy grieves, on slender accident.   180
This world is not for aye, nor 'tis not strange
That even our loves should with our fortunes change,
For 'tis a question left us yet to prove,
Whether love lead fortune, or else fortune love.
The great man down, you mark his favourite flies;   185
The poor advanced makes friends of enemies,
And hitherto doth love on fortune tend;
For who not needs shall never lack a friend,
And who in want a hollow friend doth try
Directly seasons him his enemy.   190
But orderly to end where I begun,
Our wills and fates do so contrary run
That our devices still are overthrown;
Our thoughts are ours, their ends none of our own.
So think thou wilt no second husband wed,   195
But die thy thoughts when thy first lord is dead.
PLAYER QUEEN Nor earth to me give food, nor heaven light,
Sport and repose lock from me day and night,
[To desperation turn my trust and hope,
An anchor's cheer in prison be my scope,]   200
Each opposite that blanks the face of joy
Meet what I would have well, and it destroy;
Both here and hence pursue me lasting strife,
If once a widow, ever I be wife.

HAMLET If she should break it now!   205

PLAYER KING 'Tis deeply sworn. Sweet, leave me here awhile;
My spirits grow dull, and fain I would beguile
The tedious day with sleep.
                         Sleeps
PLAYER QUEEN   Sleep rock thy brain,
And never come mischance between us twain.   *Exit*
HAMLET Madam, how like you this play?   210

GERTRUDE The lady doth protest too much methinks.

HAMLET Oh but she'll keep her word.

CLAUDIUS Have you heard the argument? Is there no offence in't?

HAMLET No, no, they do but jest, poison in jest, no offence i'th'world.

CLAUDIUS What do you call the play?   215

HAMLET The Mousetrap. Marry how? Tropically. This play is the
   image of a murder done in Vienna. Gonzago is the duke's name,
   his wife Baptista. You shall see anon. 'Tis a knavish piece of work,
   but what o' that? Your majesty, and we that have free souls, it
   touches us not. Let the galled jade winch, our withers are unwrung.   220

Enter LUCIANUS

   This is one Lucianus, nephew to the king.

OPHELIA You are as good as a chorus my lord.

HAMLET I could interpret between you and your love if I could see the
   puppets dallying.

OPHELIA You are keen my lord, you are keen.   225

HAMLET It would cost you a groaning to take off mine edge.

OPHELIA Still better and worse.

HAMLET So you mistake your husbands. Begin, murderer. Pox, leave
   thy damnable faces and begin. Come, the croaking raven doth
   bellow for revenge.   230

LUCIANUS Thoughts black, hands apt, drugs fit, and time agreeing,
        Confederate season, else no creature seeing.
        Thou mixture rank, of midnight weeds collected,
        With Hecat's ban thrice blasted, thrice infected,
        Thy natural magic and dire property   235
        On wholesome life usurp immediately.
                Pours the poison in his ears

HAMLET A poisons him i'th'garden for's estate. His name's Gonzago.
   The story is extant, and written in very choice Italian. You shall
   see anon how the murderer gets the love of Gonzago's wife.

OPHELIA The king riscs.   240

HAMLET What, frighted with false fire?

GERTRUDE How fares my lord?

POLONIUS Give o'er the play.

CLAUDIUS Give me some light. Away!

LORDS Lights, lights, lights!   245

                Exeunt all but Hamlet and Horatio

HAMLET Why, let the strucken deer go weep,
　　　　　The hart ungallèd play,
　　　　For some must watch while some must sleep,
　　　　　Thus runs the world away.
　　　Would not this, sir, and a forest of feathers, if the rest of my fortunes   250
　　　turn Turk with me, with two provincial roses on my razed shoes,
　　　get me a fellowship in a cry of players, sir?

HORATIO Half a share.

HAMLET A whole one I.
　　　　　For thou dost know, O Damon dear,   255
　　　　　　This realm dismantled was
　　　　　Of Jove himself, and now reigns here
　　　　　A very, very – pajock.

HORATIO You might have rhymed.

HAMLET O good Horatio, I'll take the ghost's word for a thousand   260
　　　pound. Didst perceive?

HORATIO Very well my lord.

HAMLET Upon the talk of the poisoning?

HORATIO I did very well note him.

Enter ROSENCRANTZ *and* GUILDENSTERN

HAMLET Ah ha! – Come, some music! Come, the recorders!   265
　　　　　For if the king like not the comedy,
　　　　　Why then – belike he likes it not, perdy.
　　　Come, some music!

GUILDENSTERN Good my lord, vouchsafe me a word with you.

HAMLET Sir, a whole history.   270

GUILDENSTERN The king, sir –

HAMLET Ay sir, what of him?

GUILDENSTERN Is in his retirement marvellous distempered.

HAMLET With drink sir?

GUILDENSTERN No my lord, rather with choler.   275

HAMLET Your wisdom should show itself more richer to signify this
　　　to his doctor, for, for me to put him to his purgation would perhaps
　　　plunge him into far more choler.

GUILDENSTERN Good my lord, put your discourse into some frame,
　　　and start not so wildly from my affair.   280

HAMLET I am tame sir, pronounce.

GUILDENSTERN The queen your mother, in most great affliction of
　　　spirit, hath sent me to you.

HAMLET You are welcome.

GUILDENSTERN Nay good my lord, this courtesy is not of the right   285
    breed. If it shall please you to make me a wholesome answer, I will
    do your mother's commandment. If not, your pardon and my return
    shall be the end of my business.

HAMLET Sir, I cannot.

ROSENCRANTZ What, my lord?   290

HAMLET Make you a wholesome answer; my wit's diseased. But, sir,
    such answer as I can make, you shall command, or rather, as you
    say, my mother. Therefore no more, but to the matter. My mother,
    you say.

ROSENCRANTZ Then thus she says. Your behaviour hath struck her   295
    into amazement and admiration.

HAMLET O wonderful son that can so stonish a mother! But is there
    no sequel at the heels of this mother's admiration? Impart.

ROSENCRANTZ She desires to speak with you in her closet ere you go
    to bed.   300

HAMLET We shall obey, were she ten times our mother. Have you any
    further trade with us?

ROSENCRANTZ My lord, you once did love me.

HAMLET And do still, by these pickers and stealers.

ROSENCRANTZ Good my lord, what is your cause of distemper? You   305
    do surely bar the door upon your own liberty if you deny your griefs
    to your friend.

HAMLET Sir, I lack advancement.

ROSENCRANTZ How can that be, when you have the voice of the king
    himself for your succession in Denmark?   310

HAMLET Ay sir, but while the grass grows – the proverb is something
    musty.

Enter the PLAYERS *with recorders*

    Oh, the recorders. Let me see one. To withdraw with you – Why
    do you go about to recover the wind of me, as if you would drive
    me into a toil?   315

GUILDENSTERN O my lord, if my duty be too bold, my love is too
    unmannerly.

HAMLET I do not well understand that. Will you play upon this pipe?

GUILDENSTERN My lord, I cannot.

HAMLET I pray you.   320

GUILDENSTERN Believe me I cannot.

HAMLET I do beseech you.

GUILDENSTERN I know no touch of it my lord.

HAMLET 'Tis as easy as lying. Govern these ventages with your fingers
and thumb, give it breath with your mouth, and it will discourse   325
most eloquent music. Look you, these are the stops.

GUILDENSTERN But these cannot I command to any utterance of
harmony. I have not the skill.

HAMLET Why look you now how unworthy a thing you make of me.
You would play upon me, you would seem to know my stops, you   330
would pluck out the heart of my mystery, you would sound me from
my lowest note to the top of my compass – and there is much music,
excellent voice, in this little organ, yet cannot you make it speak.
'Sblood, do you think I am easier to be played on than a pipe? Call
me what instrument you will, though you can fret me, you cannot   335
play upon me.

Enter POLONIUS

God bless you sir.

POLONIUS My lord, the queen would speak with you, and presently.

HAMLET Do you see yonder cloud that's almost in shape of a camel?

POLONIUS By th'mass, and 'tis like a camel indeed.   340

HAMLET Methinks it is like a weasel.

POLONIUS It is backed like a weasel.

HAMLET Or like a whale?

POLONIUS Very like a whale.

HAMLET Then I will come to my mother by and by. – They fool me   345
to the top of my bent. – I will come by and by.

POLONIUS I will say so.   *Exit*

HAMLET By and by is easily said. – Leave me, friends.

Exeunt all but Hamlet

'Tis now the very witching time of night,
When churchyards yawn, and hell itself breathes out   350
Contagion to this world. Now could I drink hot blood,
And do such bitter business as the day
Would quake to look on. Soft, now to my mother.
O heart, lose not thy nature; let not ever
The soul of Nero enter this firm bosom.   355
Let me be cruel, not unnatural:
I will speak daggers to her but use none.
My tongue and soul in this be hypocrites,
How in my words somever she be shent,
To give them seals never my soul consent.   *Exit* 360

[3.3] *Enter* CLAUDIUS, ROSENCRANTZ *and* GUILDENSTERN

CLAUDIUS I like him not, nor stands it safe with us
    To let his madness range. Therefore prepare you:
    I your commission will forthwith dispatch,
    And he to England shall along with you.
    The terms of our estate may not endure   5
    Hazard so near us as doth hourly grow
    Out of his brows.
GUILDENSTERN   We will ourselves provide.
    Most holy and religious fear it is
    To keep those many many bodies safe
    That live and feed upon your majesty.   10
ROSENCRANTZ The single and peculiar life is bound
    With all the strength and armour of the mind
    To keep itself from noyance; but much more
    That spirit upon whose weal depends and rests
    The lives of many. The cess of majesty   15
    Dies not alone, but like a gulf doth draw
    What's near it with it. It is a massy wheel
    Fixed on the summit of the highest mount,
    To whose huge spokes ten thousand lesser things
    Are mortised and adjoined, which when it falls, 20
    Each small annexment, petty consequence,
    Attends the boisterous ruin. Never alone
    Did the king sigh, but with a general groan.
CLAUDIUS Arm you I pray you to this speedy voyage,
    For we will fetters put about this fear   25
    Which now goes too free-footed.
ROSENCRANTZ   We will haste us.
         Exeunt Rosencrantz and Guildenstern

Enter POLONIUS

POLONIUS My lord, he's going to his mother's closet.
    Behind the arras I'll convey myself
    To hear the process. I'll warrant she'll tax him home,
    And as you said, and wisely was it said,   30
    'Tis meet that some more audience than a mother,
    Since nature makes them partial, should o'erhear
    The speech of vantage. Fare you well my liege,
    I'll call upon you ere you go to bed

And tell you what I know.

CLAUDIUS   Thanks, dear my lord.   35

Exit Polonius

Oh my offence is rank, it smells to heaven;
It hath the primal eldest curse upon't,
A brother's murder. Pray can I not,
Though inclination be as sharp as will.
My stronger guilt defeats my strong intent,   40
And like a man to double business bound,
I stand in pause where I shall first begin,
And both neglect. What if this cursèd hand
Were thicker than itself with brother's blood,
Is there not rain enough in the sweet heavens   45
To wash it white as snow? Whereto serves mercy
But to confront the visage of offence?
And what's in prayer but this two-fold force,
To be forestallèd ere we come to fall,
Or pardoned being down? Then I'll look up,   50
My fault is past. But oh, what form of prayer
Can serve my turn? 'Forgive me my foul murder'?
That cannot be, since I am still possessed
Of those effects for which I did the murder,
My crown, mine own ambition, and my queen.   55
May one be pardoned and retain th'offence?
In the corrupted currents of this world
Offence's gilded hand may shove by justice,
And oft 'tis seen the wicked prize itself
Buys out the law. But 'tis not so above;   60
There is no shuffling, there the action lies
In his true nature, and we ourselves compelled
Even to the teeth and forehead of our faults
To give in evidence. What then? What rests?
Try what repentance can. What can it not?   65
Yet what can it when one cannot repent?
Oh wretched state! Oh bosom black as death!
Oh limèd soul that struggling to be free
Art more engaged! Help, angels! – Make assay:
Bow stubborn knees, and heart with strings of steel   70
Be soft as sinews of the new-born babe.
All may be well.

                      [He kneels]

Enter HAMLET

HAMLET Now might I do it pat, now a is a-praying,
              And now I'll do't – and so a goes to heaven,
              And so am I revenged. That would be scanned.   75
              A villain kills my father, and for that,
              I his sole son do this same villain send
              To heaven.
              Why, this is hire and salary, not revenge.
              A took my father grossly, full of bread,   80
              With all his crimes broad blown, as flush as May,
              And how his audit stands who knows save heaven?
              But in our circumstance and course of thought
              'Tis heavy with him. And am I then revenged
              To take him in the purging of his soul,   85
              When he is fit and seasoned for his passage?
              No.
              Up sword, and know thou a more horrid hent,
              When he is drunk asleep, or in his rage,
              Or in th'incestuous pleasure of his bed,   90
              At game a-swearing, or about some act
              That has no relish of salvation in't –
              Then trip him that his heels may kick at heaven,
              And that his soul may be as damned and black
              As hell whereto it goes. My mother stays.   95
              This physic but prolongs thy sickly days.   *Exit*
CLAUDIUS My words fly up, my thoughts remain below.
              Words without thoughts never to heaven go.   *Exit*

[3.4] *Enter* GERTRUDE *and* POLONIUS

POLONIUS A will come straight. Look you lay home to him.
              Tell him his pranks have been too broad to bear with,
              And that your grace hath screened and stood between
              Much heat and him. I'll silence me e'en here.
              Pray you be round with him.   5
HAMLET (*Within*) Mother, mother, mother!
GERTRUDE I'll warrant you, fear me not. Withdraw, I hear him coming.
              [*Polonius hides himself behind the arras*]

Enter HAMLET

HAMLET Now mother, what's the matter?

GERTRUDE Hamlet, thou hast thy father much offended.

HAMLET Mother, you have my father much offended.   10

GERTRUDE Come, come, you answer with an idle tongue.

HAMLET Go, go, you question with a wicked tongue.

GERTRUDE Why, how now Hamlet?

HAMLET   What's the matter now?

GERTRUDE Have you forgot me?

HAMLET   No by the rood, not so.
      You are the queen, your husband's brother's wife,   15
      And, would it were not so, you are my mother.

GERTRUDE Nay, then I'll set those to you that can speak.

HAMLET Come, come and sit you down, you shall not budge.
      You go not till I set you up a glass
      Where you may see the inmost part of you.   20

GERTRUDE What wilt thou do? thou wilt not murder me?
      Help, help, ho!

POLONIUS (*Behind*) What ho! Help, help, help!

HAMLET (*Draws*) How now, a rat? Dead for a ducat, dead.

               Kills Polonius

POLONIUS (*Behind*) Oh, I am slain!

GERTRUDE   Oh me, what hast thou done?   25

HAMLET Nay I know not, is it the king?

GERTRUDE Oh what a rash and bloody deed is this!

HAMLET A bloody deed? Almost as bad, good mother,
      As kill a king and marry with his brother.

GERTRUDE As kill a king?

HAMLET   Ay lady, 'twas my word.   30
      [*Lifts up the arras and reveals the body of Polonius*]
      Thou wretched, rash, intruding fool, farewell.
      I took thee for thy better. Take thy fortune.
      Thou find'st to be too busy is some danger. –
      Leave wringing of your hands. Peace! Sit you down
      And let me wring your heart, for so I shall   35
      If it be made of penetrable stuff,
      If damnèd custom have not brazed it so,
      That it be proof and bulwark against sense.

GERTRUDE What have I done, that thou dar'st wag thy tongue
      In noise so rude against me?

HAMLET   Such an act   40
      That blurs the grace and blush of modesty,

Calls virtue hypocrite, takes off the rose
From the fair forehead of an innocent love
And sets a blister there, makes marriage vows
As false as dicers' oaths. Oh such a deed   45
As from the body of contraction plucks
The very soul, and sweet religion makes
A rhapsody of words. Heaven's face doth glow;
Yea, this solidity and compound mass,
With tristful visage as against the doom,   50
Is thought-sick at the act.

GERTRUDE   Ay me, what act,
That roars so loud and thunders in the index?

HAMLET Look here upon this picture, and on this,
The counterfeit presentment of two brothers.
See what a grace was seated on this brow;   55
Hyperion's curls, the front of Jove himself,
An eye like Mars, to threaten and command;
A station like the herald Mercury,
New-lighted on a heaven-kissing hill;
A combination and a form indeed,   60
Where every god did seem to set his seal
To give the world assurance of a man.
This was your husband. Look you now what follows.
Here is your husband, like a mildewed ear
Blasting his wholesome brother. Have you eyes?   65
Could you on this fair mountain leave to feed
And batten on this moor? Ha! have you eyes?
You cannot call it love, for at your age
The heyday in the blood is tame, it's humble,
And waits upon the judgement; and what judgement   70
Would step from this to this? [Sense sure you have,
Else could you not have motion, but sure that sense
Is apoplexed, for madness would not err,
Nor sense to ecstasy was ne'er so thralled,
But it reserved some quantity of choice   75
To serve in such a difference.] What devil was't
That thus hath cozened you at hoodman-blind?
[Eyes without feeling, feeling without sight,
Ears without hands or eyes, smelling sans all,
Or but a sickly part of one true sense   80
Could not so mope.]

O shame, where is thy blush? Rebellious hell,
If thou canst mutine in a matron's bones,
To flaming youth let virtue be as wax
And melt in her own fire. Proclaim no shame   85
When the compulsive ardour gives the charge,
Since frost itself as actively doth burn,
And reason panders will.

GERTRUDE   O Hamlet, speak no more.
Thou turn'st my eyes into my very soul,
And there I see such black and grainèd spots   90
As will not leave their tinct.

HAMLET   Nay, but to live
In the rank sweat of an enseamèd bed,
Stewed in corruption, honeying and making love
Over the nasty sty.

GERTRUDE   Oh speak to me no more.
These words like daggers enter in my ears.   95
No more sweet Hamlet.

HAMLET   A murderer and a villain,
A slave that is not twentieth part the tithe
Of your precedent lord, a vice of kings,
A cutpurse of the empire and the rule,
That from a shelf the precious diadem stole   100
And put it in his pocket.

GERTRUDE   No more!

Enter GHOST

HAMLET A king of shreds and patches –
Save me and hover o'er me with your wings,
You heavenly guards! – What would your gracious figure?

GERTRUDE Alas he's mad!   105

HAMLET Do you not come your tardy son to chide,
That lapsed in time and passion lets go by
Th'important acting of your dread command? Oh say!

GHOST Do not forget. This visitation
Is but to whet thy almost blunted purpose.   110
But look, amazement on thy mother sits.
Oh step between her and her fighting soul:
Conceit in weakest bodies strongest works.
Speak to her, Hamlet.

HAMLET   How is it with you lady?

GERTRUDE Alas, how is't with you, 115
      That you do bend your eye on vacancy,
      And with th'incorporal air do hold discourse?
      Forth at your eyes your spirits wildly peep,
      And, as the sleeping soldiers in th'alarm,
      Your bedded hair, like life in excrements, 120
      Start up and stand an end. O gentle son,
      Upon the heat and flame of thy distemper
      Sprinkle cool patience. Whereon do you look?
HAMLET On him, on him! Look you how pale he glares.
      His form and cause conjoined, preaching to stones, 125
      Would make them capable. – Do not look upon me,
      Lest with this piteous action you convert
      My stern effects. Then what I have to do
      Will want true colour: tears perchance for blood.
GERTRUDE To whom do you speak this? 130
HAMLET Do you see nothing there?
GERTRUDE Nothing at all, yet all that is I see.
HAMLET Nor did you nothing hear?
GERTRUDE No, nothing but ourselves.
HAMLET Why, look you there – look how it steals away – 135
      My father in his habit as he lived –
      Look where he goes, even now out at the portal.

                              Exit Ghost

GERTRUDE This is the very coinage of your brain.
      This bodiless creation ecstasy
      Is very cunning in.
HAMLET   Ecstasy? 140
      My pulse as yours doth temperately keep time,
      And makes as healthful music. It is not madness
      That I have uttered. Bring me to the test,
      And I the matter will reword, which madness
      Would gambol from. Mother, for love of grace, 145
      Lay not that flattering unction to your soul,
      That not your trespass but my madness speaks;
      It will but skin and film the ulcerous place,
      Whiles rank corruption, mining all within,
      Infects unseen. Confess yourself to heaven, 150
      Repent what's past, avoid what is to come,
      And do not spread the compost on the weeds
      To make them ranker. Forgive me this my virtue,

        For in the fatness of these pursy times
        Virtue itself of vice must pardon beg,   155
        Yea, curb and woo for leave to do him good.
GERTRUDE Oh Hamlet, thou hast cleft my heart in twain.
HAMLET Oh throw away the worser part of it
        And live the purer with the other half.
        Good night – but go not to my uncle's bed;   160
        Assume a virtue if you have it not.
        [That monster custom, who all sense doth eat,
        Of habits devil, is angel yet in this,
        That to the use of actions fair and good
        He likewise gives a frock or livery   165
        That aptly is put on.] Refrain tonight,
        And that shall lend a kind of easiness
        To the next abstinence, [the next more easy,
        For use almost can change the stamp of nature,
        And either . . . the devil, or throw him out,   170
        With wondrous potency.] Once more good night,
        And when you are desirous to be blessed,
        I'll blessing beg of you. For this same lord,
        I do repent; but heaven hath pleased it so,
        To punish me with this, and this with me,   175
        That I must be their scourge and minister.
        I will bestow him, and will answer well
        The death I gave him. So again, good night.
        I must be cruel only to be kind;
        Thus bad begins, and worse remains behind.   180
        One word more good lady.
GERTRUDE   What shall I do?
HAMLET Not this by no means that I bid you do:
        Let the bloat king tempt you again to bed,
        Pinch wanton on your cheek, call you his mouse,
        And let him for a pair of reechy kisses,   185
        Or paddling in your neck with his damned fingers,
        Make you to ravel all this matter out,
        That I essentially am not in madness,
        But mad in craft. 'Twere good you let him know,
        For who that's but a queen, fair, sober, wise,   190
        Would from a paddock, from a bat, a gib,
        Such dear concernings hide? Who would do so?
        No, in despite of sense and secrecy,

    Unpeg the basket on the house's top,
    Let the birds fly, and like the famous ape,   195
    To try conclusions, in the basket creep
    And break your own neck down.
GERTRUDE Be thou assured, if words be made of breath,
    And breath of life, I have no life to breathe
    What thou hast said to me.   200
HAMLET I must to England, you know that?
GERTRUDE   Alack,
    I had forgot. 'Tis so concluded on.
HAMLET [There's letters sealed, and my two schoolfellows,
    Whom I will trust as I will adders fanged,
    They bear the mandate. They must sweep my way   205
    And marshal me to knavery. Let it work,
    For 'tis the sport to have the engineer
    Hoist with his own petar, an't shall go hard
    But I will delve one yard below their mines
    And blow them at the moon. Oh 'tis most sweet   210
    When in one line two crafts directly meet.]
    This man shall set me packing.
    I'll lug the guts into the neighbour room.
    Mother, good night. Indeed, this counsellor
    Is now most still, most secret, and most grave,   215
    Who was in life a foolish prating knave.
    Come sir, to draw toward an end with you.
    Good night mother.
     Exit Hamlet tugging in Polonius; [*Gertrude remains*]

[4.1] *Enter* CLAUDIUS *with* ROSENCRANTZ *and* GUILDENSTERN

CLAUDIUS There's matter in these sighs, these profound heaves.
    You must translate, 'tis fit we understand them.
    Where is your son?
GERTRUDE [Bestow this place on us a little while.]
                   [*Exeunt Rosencrantz and Guildenstern*]
    Ah mine own lord, what have I seen tonight!   5
CLAUDIUS What, Gertrude? How does Hamlet?
GERTRUDE Mad as the sea and wind, when both contend
    Which is the mightier. In his lawless fit,
    Behind the arras hearing something stir,

| | Whips out his rapier, cries 'A rat, a rat!', | 10 |

Whips out his rapier, cries 'A rat, a rat!',   10
And in this brainish apprehension kills
The unseen good old man.

CLAUDIUS   Oh heavy deed!
It had been so with us had we been there.
His liberty is full of threats to all,
To you yourself, to us, to everyone.   15
Alas, how shall this bloody deed be answered?
It will be laid to us, whose providence
Should have kept short, restrained, and out of haunt,
This mad young man. But so much was our love,
We would not understand what was most fit,   20
But like the owner of a foul disease,
To keep it from divulging, let it feed
Even on the pith of life. Where is he gone?

GERTRUDE To draw apart the body he hath killed,
O'er whom his very madness, like some ore   25
Among a mineral of metals base,
Shows itself pure; a weeps for what is done.

CLAUDIUS Oh Gertrude, come away!
The sun no sooner shall the mountains touch
But we will ship him hence, and this vile deed   30
We must with all our majesty and skill
Both countenance and excuse. Ho, Guildenstern!

                Enter ROSENCRANTZ *and* GUILDENSTERN

Friends both, go join you with some further aid.
Hamlet in madness hath Polonius slain,
And from his mother's closet hath he dragged him.   35
Go seek him out, speak fair, and bring the body
Into the chapel. I pray you haste in this.

                Exeunt Rosencrantz and Guildenstern

Come Gertrude, we'll call up our wisest friends
And let them know both what we mean to do
And what's untimely done.   40
[Whose whisper o'er the world's diameter,
As level as the cannon to his blank,
Transports his poisoned shot, may miss our name
And hit the woundless air.] Oh come away,
My soul is full of discord and dismay.   45

                                                        Exeunt

[4.2] *Enter* HAMLET

HAMLET Safely stowed.
GENTLEMEN (*Within*) Hamlet! Lord Hamlet!
HAMLET But soft, what noise? Who calls on Hamlet? Oh here they
come.

Enter ROSENCRANTZ *and* GUILDENSTERN

ROSENCRANTZ What have you done my lord with the dead body?   5
HAMLET Compounded it with dust whereto 'tis kin.
ROSENCRANTZ Tell us where 'tis, that we may take it thence and bear
it to the chapel.
HAMLET Do not believe it.
ROSENCRANTZ Believe what?   10
HAMLET That I can keep your counsel and not mine own. Besides, to
be demanded of a sponge, what replication should be made by the
son of a king?
ROSENCRANTZ Take you me for a sponge my lord?
HAMLET Ay sir, that soaks up the king's countenance, his rewards, his   15
authorities. But such officers do the king best service in the end:
he keeps them like an ape in the corner of his jaw, first mouthed
to be last swallowed. When he needs what you have gleaned, it is
but squeezing you, and, sponge, you shall be dry again.
ROSENCRANTZ I understand you not my lord.   20
HAMLET I am glad of it, a knavish speech sleeps in a foolish ear.
ROSENCRANTZ My lord, you must tell us where the body is, and go
with us to the king.
HAMLET The body is with the king, but the king is not with the body.
The king is a thing –   25
GUILDENSTERN A thing my lord?
HAMLET Of nothing. Bring me to him. Hide fox, and all after!
Exeunt

[4.3] *Enter* CLAUDIUS, *and two or three*

CLAUDIUS I have sent to seek him, and to find the body.
How dangerous is it that this man goes loose,
Yet must not we put the strong law on him;
He's loved of the distracted multitude,
Who like not in their judgement, but their eyes;   5

And where 'tis so, th'offender's scourge is weighed,
But never the offence. To bear all smooth and even,
This sudden sending him away must seem
Deliberate pause. Diseases desperate grown
By desperate appliance are relieved,   10
Or not at all.

Enter ROSENCRANTZ

How now, what hath befallen?

ROSENCRANTZ Where the dead body is bestowed, my lord,
We cannot get from him.

CLAUDIUS   But where is he?

ROSENCRANTZ Without, my lord, guarded, to know your pleasure.

CLAUDIUS Bring him before us.

ROSENCRANTZ   Ho! bring in my lord.   15

Enter HAMLET *and* GUILDENSTERN

CLAUDIUS Now Hamlet, where's Polonius?

HAMLET At supper.

CLAUDIUS At supper? Where?

HAMLET Not where he eats, but where a is eaten. A certain convocation
of politic worms are e'en at him. Your worm is your only emperor   20
for diet: we fat all creatures else to fat us, and we fat ourselves for
maggots. Your fat king and your lean beggar is but variable service,
two dishes, but to one table; that's the end.

CLAUDIUS Alas, alas.

HAMLET A man may fish with the worm that hath eat of a king, and   25
eat of the fish that hath fed of that worm.

CLAUDIUS What dost thou mean by this?

HAMLET Nothing but to show you how a king may go a progress
through the guts of a beggar.

CLAUDIUS Where is Polonius?   30

HAMLET In heaven, send thither to see. If your messenger find him not
there, seek him i'th'other place yourself. But if indeed you find him
not within this month, you shall nose him as you go up the stairs
into the lobby.

CLAUDIUS Go seek him there.   35

HAMLET A will stay till you come.

                                        [*Exeunt Attendants*]

CLAUDIUS Hamlet, this deed, for thine especial safety,
Which we do tender, as we dearly grieve

For that which thou hast done, must send thee hence
With fiery quickness. Therefore prepare thyself.   40
The bark is ready and the wind at help,
Th'associates tend, and everything is bent
For England.

HAMLET   For England?
CLAUDIUS   Ay Hamlet.
HAMLET   Good.
CLAUDIUS So is it if thou knew'st our purposes.
HAMLET I see a cherub that sees them. But come, for England! Farewell   45
  dear mother.
CLAUDIUS Thy loving father, Hamlet.
HAMLET My mother. Father and mother is man and wife, man and wife
  is one flesh, and so, my mother. Come, for England.   *Exit*
CLAUDIUS Follow him at foot, tempt him with speed aboard.   50
  Delay it not, I'll have him hence tonight.
  Away, for everything is sealed and done
  That else leans on th'affair. Pray you make haste.
            [*Exeunt Rosencrantz and Guildenstern*]
  And England, if my love thou hold'st at aught,
  As my great power thereof may give thee sense,   55
  Since yet thy cicatrice looks raw and red
  After the Danish sword, and thy free awe
  Pays homage to us – thou mayst not coldly set
  Our sovereign process, which imports at full,
  By letters congruing to that effect,   60
  The present death of Hamlet. Do it England,
  For like the hectic in my blood he rages,
  And thou must cure me. Till I know 'tis done,
  Howe'er my haps, my joys were ne'er begun.   *Exit*

[4.4] *Enter* FORTINBRAS *with his army over the stage*

FORTINBRAS Go captain, from me greet the Danish king.
  Tell him that by his licence, Fortinbras
  Craves the conveyance of a promised march
  Over his kingdom. You know the rendezvous.
  If that his majesty would aught with us,   5
  We shall express our duty in his eye,
  And let him know so.

CAPTAIN   I will do't, my lord.
FORTINBRAS Go softly on.

                                [Exit Fortinbras, with the army]

                Enter HAMLET, ROSENCRANTZ, *etc.*

HAMLET Good sir, whose powers are these?
CAPTAIN They are of Norway sir.   10
HAMLET How purposed sir I pray you?
CAPTAIN Against some part of Poland.
HAMLET Who commands them sir?
CAPTAIN The nephew to old Norway, Fortinbras.
HAMLET Goes it against the main of Poland sir,   15
        Or for some frontier?
CAPTAIN Truly to speak, and with no addition,
        We go to gain a little patch of ground
        That hath in it no profit but the name.
        To pay five ducats, five, I would not farm it,   20
        Nor will it yield to Norway or the Pole
        A ranker rate, should it be sold in fee.
HAMLET Why then the Polack never will defend it.
CAPTAIN Yes, it is already garrisoned.
HAMLET Two thousand souls and twenty thousand ducats   25
        Will not debate the question of this straw.
        This is th'impostume of much wealth and peace,
        That inward breaks, and shows no cause without
        Why the man dies. I humbly thank you sir.
CAPTAIN God buy you sir.   *[Exit]*
ROSENCRANTZ   Will't please you go my lord?   30
HAMLET I'll be with you straight; go a little before.

                       [Exeunt all but Hamlet]
        How all occasions do inform against me,
        And spur my dull revenge! What is a man
        If his chief good and market of his time
        Be but to sleep and feed? A beast, no more.   35
        Sure he that made us with such large discourse,
        Looking before and after, gave us not
        That capability and god-like reason
        To fust in us unused. Now whether it be
        Bestial oblivion, or some craven scruple   40
        Of thinking too precisely on th'event –
        A thought which quartered hath but one part wisdom

And ever three parts coward – I do not know
Why yet I live to say this thing's to do,
Sith I have cause, and will, and strength, and means   45
To do't. Examples gross as earth exhort me.
Witness this army of such mass and charge,
Led by a delicate and tender prince,
Whose spirit with divine ambition puffed
Makes mouths at the invisible event,   50
Exposing what is mortal and unsure
To all that fortune, death and danger dare,
Even for an egg-shell. Rightly to be great
Is not to stir without great argument,
But greatly to find quarrel in a straw   55
When honour's at the stake. How stand I then,
That have a father killed, a mother stained,
Excitements of my reason and my blood,
And let all sleep, while to my shame I see
The imminent death of twenty thousand men,   60
That for a fantasy and trick of fame
Go to their graves like beds, fight for a plot
Whereon the numbers cannot try the cause,
Which is not tomb enough and continent
To hide the slain. Oh from this time forth,   65
My thoughts be bloody or be nothing worth.   *Exit*

[4.5] *Enter* HORATIO, GERTRUDE *and a* GENTLEMAN

GERTRUDE I will not speak with her.
GENTLEMAN She is importunate, indeed distract;
  Her mood will needs be pitied.
GERTRUDE   What would she have?
GENTLEMAN She speaks much of her father, says she hears
  There's tricks i'th'world, and hems, and beats her heart,   5
  Spurns enviously at straws, speaks things in doubt
  That carry but half sense. Her speech is nothing,
  Yet the unshapèd use of it doth move
  The hearers to collection. They yawn at it,
  And botch the words up fit to their own thoughts,   10
  Which, as her winks and nods and gestures yield them,

  Indeed would make one think there might be thought,
  Though nothing sure, yet much unhappily.
HORATIO 'Twere good she were spoken with, for she may strew
  Dangerous conjectures in ill-breeding minds.   15
GERTRUDE Let her come in.

             [Exit Gentleman]

  (*Aside*) To my sick soul, as sin's true nature is,
  Each toy seems prologue to some great amiss.
  So full of artless jealousy is guilt,
  It spills itself in fearing to be spilt.   20

     Enter OPHELIA *distracted*

OPHELIA Where is the beauteous majesty of Denmark?
GERTRUDE How now Ophelia?
OPHELIA   *She sings*
    How should I your true love know
     From another one?
    By his cockle hat and staff   25
     And his sandal shoon.
GERTRUDE Alas sweet lady, what imports this song?
OPHELIA Say you? Nay, pray you mark.
    He is dead and gone lady,   *Song*
     He is dead and gone;   30
    At his head a grass green turf,
     At his heels a stone.
 Oho!
GERTRUDE Nay but Ophelia –
OPHELIA Pray you mark.   35
    White his shroud as the mountain snow – *Song*

     Enter CLAUDIUS

GERTRUDE Alas, look here my lord.
OPHELIA   Larded all with sweet flowers,
     Which bewept to the grave did not go
    With true-love showers.   40
CLAUDIUS How do you, pretty lady?
OPHELIA Well good dild you. They say the owl was a baker's daughter.
 Lord, we know what we are, but know not what we may be. God
 be at your table.
CLAUDIUS Conceit upon her father.   45

OPHELIA Pray let's have no words of this, but when they ask you what
 it means, say you this –

    Tomorrow is Saint Valentine's day,   *Song*
     All in the morning betime,
    And I a maid at your window,   50
     To be your Valentine.

    Then up he rose and donned his clothes
     And dupped the chamber door;
    Let in the maid that out a maid
     Never departed more.   55

CLAUDIUS Pretty Ophelia!

OPHELIA Indeed la! Without an oath I'll make an end on't.
    By Gis and by Saint Charity,
     Alack and fie for shame,
    Young men will do't if they come to't –   60
     By Cock, they are to blame.

    Quoth she, 'Before you tumbled me,
     You promised me to wed.'

He answers –

    So would I ha' done, by yonder sun,   65
     And thou hadst not come to my bed.

CLAUDIUS How long hath she been thus?

OPHELIA I hope all will be well. We must be patient, but I cannot
 choose but weep to think they would lay him i'th' cold ground. My
 brother shall know of it, and so I thank you for your good counsel. 70
 Come, my coach. Good night ladies, good night sweet ladies, good
 night, good night.   *Exit*

CLAUDIUS Follow her close, give her good watch I pray you.
                [*Exit Horatio*]
    Oh this is the poison of deep grief, it springs
    All from her father's death, [and now behold –] 75
    Oh Gertrude, Gertrude,
    When sorrows come, they come not single spies,
    But in battalions. First, her father slain;
    Next, your son gone, and he most violent author
    Of his own just remove; the people muddied,   80

Thick and unwholesome in their thoughts and whispers
For good Polonius' death – and we have done but greenly
In hugger-mugger to inter him; poor Ophelia
Divided from herself and her fair judgement,
Without the which we are pictures, or mere beasts;   85
Last, and as much containing as all these,
Her brother is in secret come from France,
Feeds on his wonder, keeps himself in clouds,
And wants not buzzers to infect his ear
With pestilent speeches of his father's death,   90
Wherein necessity, of matter beggared,
Will nothing stick our person to arraign
In ear and ear. O my dear Gertrude, this,
Like to a murdering piece, in many places
Gives me superfluous death.   95

A noise within

GERTRUDE Alack, what noise is this?
CLAUDIUS Attend! Where are my Swissers? Let them guard the door.

Enter a MESSENGER

What is the matter?
MESSENGER   Save yourself my lord.
The ocean, overpeering of his list,
Eats not the flats with more impitious haste   100
Than young Laertes in a riotous head
O'erbears your officers. The rabble call him lord,
And, as the world were now but to begin,
Antiquity forgot, custom not known,
The ratifiers and props of every word,   105
They cry 'Choose we! Laertes shall be king.'
Caps, hands and tongues applaud it to the clouds,
'Laertes shall be king, Laertes king!'
GERTRUDE How cheerfully on the false trail they cry!
Oh this is counter, you false Danish dogs!   110
A noise within
CLAUDIUS The doors are broke.

Enter LAERTES *with others*

LAERTES Where is this king? – Sirs, stand you all without.

ALL No, let's come in.
LAERTES I pray you give me leave.
ALL We will, we will.   115
LAERTES I thank you. Keep the door.

                                              [*Exeunt followers*]
                         O thou vile king,
          Give me my father.
GERTRUDE   Calmly, good Laertes.
LAERTES That drop of blood that's calm proclaims me bastard,
          Cries cuckold to my father, brands the harlot
          Even here, between the chaste unsmirchèd brow   120
          Of my true mother.
CLAUDIUS   What is the cause, Laertes,
          That thy rebellion looks so giant-like? –
          Let him go, Gertrude, do not fear our person.
          There's such divinity doth hedge a king
          That treason can but peep to what it would,   125
          Acts little of his will. – Tell me Laertes,
          Why thou art thus incensed. – Let him go Gertrude. –
          Speak man.
LAERTES   Where is my father?
CLAUDIUS   Dead.
GERTRUDE   But not by him.
CLAUDIUS Let him demand his fill.
LAERTES How came he dead? I'll not be juggled with.   130
          To hell allegiance, vows to the blackest devil,
          Conscience and grace to the profoundest pit!
          I dare damnation. To this point I stand,
          That both the worlds I give to negligence,
          Let come what comes, only I'll be revenged   135
          Most throughly for my father.
CLAUDIUS   Who shall stay you?
LAERTES My will, not all the world.
          And for my means, I'll husband them so well,
          They shall go far with little.
CLAUDIUS   Good Laertes,
          If you desire to know the certainty   140
          Of your dear father, is't writ in your revenge
          That, soopstake, you will draw both friend and foe,
          Winner and loser?
LAERTES   None but his enemies.

CLAUDIUS Will you know them then?

LAERTES To his good friends thus wide I'll ope my arms,   145
       And like the kind life-rendering pelican,
       Repast them with my blood.

CLAUDIUS   Why now you speak
       Like a good child and a true gentleman.
       That I am guiltless of your father's death,
       And am most sensibly in grief for it,   150
       It shall as level to your judgement pierce
       As day does to your eye.
               A noise within: 'Let her come in'

LAERTES How now, what noise is that?

Enter OPHELIA

       O heat dry up my brains, tears seven times salt
       Burn out the sense and virtue of mine eye!   155
       By heaven, thy madness shall be paid with weight
       Till our scale turn the beam. O rose of May,
       Dear maid, kind sister, sweet Ophelia –
       O heavens, is't possible a young maid's wits
       Should be as mortal as an old man's life?   160
       Nature is fine in love, and where 'tis fine,
       It sends some precious instance of itself
       After the thing it loves.

OPHELIA   They bore him bare-faced on the bier   *Song*
           Hey non nonny, nonny, hey nonny,   165
           And in his grave rained many a tear –
    Fare you well my dove.

LAERTES Hadst thou thy wits, and didst persuade revenge,
       It could not move thus.

OPHELIA You must sing a-down a-down, and you call him a-down-a.   170
Oh how the wheel becomes it. It is the false steward that stole his
master's daughter.

LAERTES This nothing's more than matter.

OPHELIA There's rosemary, that's for remembrance – pray you, love,
remember – and there is pansies, that's for thoughts.   175

LAERTES A document in madness, thoughts and remembrance fitted.

OPHELIA There's fennel for you, and columbines. There's rue for you,
and here's some for me; we may call it herb of grace a Sundays.
Oh you must wear your rue with a difference. There's a daisy. I

would give you some violets, but they withered all when my father   180
died. They say a made a good end.
[Sings]
For bonny sweet Robin is all my joy.

LAERTES Thought and affliction, passion, hell itself,
       She turns to favour and to prettiness.

OPHELIA   And will a not come again?   *Song*   185
                And will a not come again?
                  No, no, he is dead,
                   Go to thy death-bed,
                He never will come again.
                His beard was as white as snow,   190
                All flaxen was his poll,
                   He is gone, he is gone,
                  And we cast away moan,
                God-a-mercy on his soul.

    And of all Christian souls, I pray God. God buy you.   *Exit*   195

LAERTES Do you see this, O God?

CLAUDIUS Laertes, I must commune with your grief,
       Or you deny me right. Go but apart,
       Make choice of whom your wisest friends you will,
       And they shall hear and judge 'twixt you and me.   200
       If by direct or by collateral hand
       They find us touched, we will our kingdom give,
       Our crown, our life, and all that we call ours,
       To you in satisfaction. But if not,
       Be you content to lend your patience to us,   205
       And we shall jointly labour with your soul
       To give it due content.

LAERTES   Let this be so.
       His means of death, his obscure funeral,
       No trophy, sword, nor hatchment o'er his bones,
       No noble rite, nor formal ostentation,
       Cry to be heard, as 'twere from heaven to earth,   210
       That I must call't in question.

CLAUDIUS   So you shall.
       And where th'offence is, let the great axe fall.
       I pray you go with me.

Exeunt

[4.6] *Enter* HORATIO *with an* ATTENDANT

HORATIO What are they that would speak with me?
ATTENDANT Seafaring men sir, they say they have letters for you.
HORATIO Let them come in.

                                        [*Exit Attendant*]

      I do not know from what part of the world
      I should be greeted, if not from Lord Hamlet.   5

                        Enter SAILORS

1 SAILOR God bless you sir.
HORATIO Let him bless thee too.
1 SAILOR A shall sir, and please him. There's a letter for you sir, it came
    from th'ambassador that was bound for England, if your name be
    Horatio, as I am let to know it is.   10
HORATIO (*Reads the letter*) 'Horatio, when thou shalt have overlooked
    this, give these fellows some means to the king; they have letters
    for him. Ere we were two days old at sea, a pirate of very warlike
    appointment gave us chase. Finding ourselves too slow of sail, we
    put on a compelled valour, and in the grapple I boarded them. On   15
    the instant they got clear of our ship, so I alone became their
    prisoner. They have dealt with me like thieves of mercy, but they
    knew what they did: I am to do a good turn for them. Let the king
    have the letters I have sent, and repair thou to me with as much
    speed as thou wouldest fly death. I have words to speak in thine   20
    ear will make thee dumb, yet are they much too light for the bore
    of the matter. These good fellows will bring thee where I am.
    Rosencrantz and Guildenstern hold their course for England. Of
    them I have much to tell thee. Farewell.

                        He that thou knowest thine,   25
                                        Hamlet.'

      Come, I will give you way for these your letters,
      And do't the speedier that you may direct me
      To him from whom you brought them.

                                        Exeunt

[4.7] *Enter* CLAUDIUS *and* LAERTES

CLAUDIUS Now must your conscience my acquittance seal,
      And you must put me in your heart for friend,

Sith you have heard, and with a knowing ear,
That he which hath your noble father slain
Pursued my life.

LAERTES   It well appears. But tell me   5
Why you proceeded not against these feats,
So crimeful and so capital in nature,
As by your safety, wisdom, all things else,
You mainly were stirred up.

CLAUDIUS   Oh for two special reasons,
Which may to you perhaps seem much unsinewed,   10
But yet to me they're strong. The queen his mother
Lives almost by his looks, and for myself,
My virtue or my plague, be it either which,
She's so conjunctive to my life and soul,
That as the star moves not but in his sphere,   15
I could not but by her. The other motive,
Why to a public count I might not go,
Is the great love the general gender bear him,
Who, dipping all his faults in their affection,
Work like the spring that turneth wood to stone,   20
Convert his gyves to graces, so that my arrows,
Too slightly timbered for so loud a wind,
Would have reverted to my bow again,
And not where I had aimed them.

LAERTES And so have I a noble father lost,   25
A sister driven into desperate terms,
Whose worth, if praises may go back again,
Stood challenger on mount of all the age
For her perfections. But my revenge will come.

CLAUDIUS Break not your sleeps for that. You must not think   30
That we are made of stuff so flat and dull
That we can let our beard be shook with danger
And think it pastime. You shortly shall hear more.
I loved your father, and we love ourself,
And that I hope will teach you to imagine –   35

Enter a MESSENGER *with letters*

How now? What news?

MESSENGER   Letters my lord from Hamlet.
This to your majesty, this to the queen.

CLAUDIUS From Hamlet? Who brought them?

MESSENGER Sailors my lord they say, I saw them not;
         They were given me by Claudio – he received them   40
         Of him that brought them.
CLAUDIUS   Laertes, you shall hear them. –
         Leave us.
                                      Exit Messenger
         [*Reads*] 'High and mighty, you shall know I am set naked on your
         kingdom. Tomorrow shall I beg leave to see your kingly eyes, when
         I shall, first asking your pardon thereunto, recount th'occasion of   45
         my sudden and more strange return.
                                          Hamlet.'
         What should this mean? Are all the rest come back?
         Or is it some abuse, and no such thing?
LAERTES Know you the hand?
CLAUDIUS   'Tis Hamlet's character. Naked?   50
         And in a postscript here he says alone.
         Can you devise me?
LAERTES I'm lost in it my lord. But let him come –
         It warms the very sickness in my heart
         That I shall live and tell him to his teeth   55
         'Thus didest thou!'
CLAUDIUS   If it be so, Laertes –
         As how should it be so? – how otherwise? –
         Will you be ruled by me?
LAERTES   Ay my lord,
         So you will not o'errule me to a peace.
CLAUDIUS To thine own peace. If he be now returned,   60
         As checking at his voyage, and that he means
         No more to undertake it, I will work him
         To an exploit, now ripe in my device,
         Under the which he shall not choose but fall,
         And for his death no wind of blame shall breathe,   65
         But even his mother shall uncharge the practice
         And call it accident.
[LAERTES   My lord, I will be ruled,
         The rather if you could devise it so
         That I might be the organ.
CLAUDIUS   It falls right.
         You have been talked of since your travel much,   70
         And that in Hamlet's hearing, for a quality
         Wherein they say you shine. Your sum of parts

Did not together pluck such envy from him
As did that one, and that in my regard
Of the unworthiest siege.

LAERTES   What part is that my lord?   75

CLAUDIUS A very riband in the cap of youth,
Yet needful too, for youth no less becomes
The light and careless livery that it wears
Than settled age his sables and his weeds
Importing health and graveness.] Two months since   80
Here was a gentleman of Normandy.
I've seen myself, and served against, the French,
And they can well on horseback, but this gallant
Had witchcraft in't. He grew unto his seat,
And to such wondrous doing brought his horse   85
As had he been incorpsed and demi-natured
With the brave beast. So far he topped my thought,
That I in forgery of shapes and tricks
Come short of what he did.

LAERTES   A Norman was't?

CLAUDIUS A Norman.   90

LAERTES Upon my life Lamord.

CLAUDIUS   The very same.

LAERTES I know him well, he is the brooch indeed
And gem of all the nation.

CLAUDIUS He made confession of you,
And gave you such a masterly report   95
For art and exercise in your defence,
And for your rapier most especial,
That he cried out 'twould be a sight indeed
If one could match you. [Th'escrimers of their nation
He swore had neither motion, guard, nor eye,   100
If you opposed them.] Sir, this report of his
Did Hamlet so envenom with his envy
That he could nothing do but wish and beg
Your sudden coming o'er to play with you.
Now out of this –

LAERTES   What out of this, my lord?   105

CLAUDIUS Laertes, was your father dear to you?
Or are you like the painting of a sorrow,
A face without a heart?

LAERTES   Why ask you this?

CLAUDIUS Not that I think you did not love your father,
           But that I know love is begun by time,   110
           And that I see, in passages of proof,
           Time qualifies the spark and fire of it.
           [There lives within the very flame of love
           A kind of wick or snuff that will abate it,
           And nothing is at a like goodness still,   115
           For goodness, growing to a plurisy,
           Dies in his own too much. That we would do,
           We should do when we would, for this 'would' changes,
           And hath abatements and delays as many
           As there are tongues, are hands, are accidents;   120
           And then this 'should' is like a spendthrift sigh,
           That hurts by easing. But to the quick of th'ulcer –]
           Hamlet comes back; what would you undertake
           To show yourself in deed your father's son
           More than in words?
LAERTES   To cut his throat i'th'church.   125
CLAUDIUS No place indeed should murder sanctuarize;
           Revenge should have no bounds. But, good Laertes,
           Will you do this, keep close within your chamber;
           Hamlet, returned, shall know you are come home;
           We'll put on those shall praise your excellence,   130
           And set a double varnish on the fame
           The Frenchman gave you; bring you in fine together,
           And wager on your heads. He being remiss,
           Most generous, and free from all contriving,
           Will not peruse the foils, so that with ease,   135
           Or with a little shuffling, you may choose
           A sword unbated, and in a pass of practice
           Requite him for your father.
LAERTES   I will do't,
           And for that purpose I'll anoint my sword.
           I bought an unction of a mountebank,   140
           So mortal that but dip a knife in it,
           Where it draws blood no cataplasm so rare,
           Collected from all simples that have virtue
           Under the moon, can save the thing from death
           That is but scratched withal. I'll touch my point   145
           With this contagion, that if I gall him slightly,
           It may be death.

CLAUDIUS   Let's further think of this,
              Weigh what convenience both of time and means
              May fit us to our shape. If this should fail,
              And that our drift look through our bad performance,   150
              'Twere better not assayed. Therefore this project
              Should have a back or second, that might hold
              If this did blast in proof. Soft, let me see.
              We'll make a solemn wager on your cunnings –
              I ha't!   155
              When in your motion you are hot and dry,
              As make your bouts more violent to that end,
              And that he calls for drink, I'll have preferred him
              A chalice for the nonce, whereon but sipping,
              If he by chance escape your venomed stuck,   160
              Our purpose may hold there. But stay, what noise?

                          Enter GERTRUDE

              How, sweet queen!
GERTRUDE One woe doth tread upon another's heel,
              So fast they follow. Your sister's drowned, Laertes.
LAERTES Drowned! Oh where?   165
GERTRUDE There is a willow grows askant a brook,
              That shows his hoar leaves in the glassy stream.
              Therewith fantastic garlands did she make,
              Of crow-flowers, nettles, daisies, and long purples,
              That liberal shepherds give a grosser name,   170
              But our cold maids do dead men's fingers call them.
              There on the pendant boughs her cronet weeds
              Clamb'ring to hang, an envious sliver broke,
              When down her weedy trophies and herself
              Fell in the weeping brook. Her clothes spread wide,   175
              And mermaid-like awhile they bore her up,
              Which time she chanted snatches of old lauds
              As one incapable of her own distress,
              Or like a creature native and indued
              Unto that element. But long it could not be   180
              Till that her garments, heavy with their drink,
              Pulled the poor wretch from her melodious lay
              To muddy death.
LAERTES   Alas, then she is drowned?
GERTRUDE Drowned, drowned.

LAERTES Too much of water hast thou, poor Ophelia,   185
                And therefore I forbid my tears. But yet
                It is our trick; nature her custom holds,
                Let shame say what it will. When these are gone,
                The woman will be out. Adieu my lord,
                I have a speech of fire that fain would blaze,   190
                But that this folly douts it.   *Exit*

CLAUDIUS   Let's follow, Gertrude.
                How much I had to do to calm his rage!
                Now fear I this will give it start again.
                Therefore let's follow.

                                                              Exeunt

[5.1] *Enter two* CLOWNS

CLOWN Is she to be buried in Christian burial, when she wilfully seeks
                her own salvation?

OTHER I tell thee she is, therefore make her grave straight. The crowner
                hath sat on her, and finds it Christian burial.

CLOWN How can that be, unless she drowned herself in her own   5
                defence?

OTHER Why, 'tis found so.

CLOWN It must be *se offendendo*, it cannot be else. For here lies the
                point: if I drown myself wittingly, it argues an act, and an act hath
                three branches – it is to act, to do, to perform. Argal, she drowned   10
                herself wittingly.

OTHER Nay, but hear you goodman delver –

CLOWN Give me leave. Here lies the water – good. Here stands the
                man – good. If the man go to this water and drown himself, it is
                will he, nill he, he goes – mark you that. But if the water come to   15
                him, and drown him, he drowns not himself. Argal, he that is not
                guilty of his own death shortens not his own life.

OTHER But is this law?

CLOWN Ay marry is't, crowner's quest law.

OTHER Will you ha' the truth on't? If this had not been a gentlewoman,   20
                she should have been buried out o' Christian burial.

CLOWN Why, there thou sayst – and the more pity that great folk
                should have countenance in this world to drown or hang themselves
                more than their even-Christen. Come, my spade; there is no ancient
                gentlemen but gardeners, ditchers, and gravemakers; they hold up   25
                Adam's profession.

OTHER Was he a gentleman?

CLOWN A was the first that ever bore arms.

OTHER Why, he had none.

CLOWN What, art a heathen? How dost thou understand the scripture? 30
The scripture says Adam digged. Could he dig without arms? I'll
put another question to thee. If thou answerest me not to the
purpose, confess thyself –

OTHER Go to!

CLOWN What is he that builds stronger than either the mason, the 35
shipwright, or the carpenter?

OTHER The gallows-maker, for that frame outlives a thousand tenants.

CLOWN I like thy wit well in good faith. The gallows does well, but
how does it well? It does well to those that do ill. Now, thou dost
ill to say the gallows is built stronger than the church; argal, the 40
gallows may do well to thee. To't again, come.

OTHER Who builds stronger than a mason, a shipwright, or a carpenter?

CLOWN Ay, tell me that, and unyoke.

OTHER Marry, now I can tell.

CLOWN To't.

OTHER Mass, I cannot tell. 45

Enter HAMLET *and* HORATIO *afar off*

CLOWN Cudgel thy brains no more about it, for your dull ass will not
mend his pace with beating; and when you are asked this question
next, say a grave-maker. The houses he makes lasts till doomsday.
Go, get thee to Yaughan, fetch me a stoup of liquor. 50

[*Exit Second Clown*]

In youth when I did love, did love, *Song*
Methought it was very sweet
To contract-o the time for-a my behove,
Oh methought there-a was nothing-a meet.

HAMLET Has this fellow no feeling of his business? A sings in 55
grave-making.

HORATIO Custom hath made it in him a property of easiness.

HAMLET 'Tis e'en so, the hand of little employment hath the daintier
sense.

CLOWN But age with his stealing steps *Song* 60
Hath clawed me in his clutch,
And hath shipped me intil the land,
As if I had never been such.

[*Throws up a skull*]

HAMLET That skull had a tongue in it, and could sing once. How the
knave jowls it to th' ground, as if 'twere Cain's jawbone, that did   65
the first murder. This might be the pate of a politician which this
ass now o'erreaches, one that would circumvent God, might it not?

HORATIO It might my lord.

HAMLET Or of a courtier, which could say 'Good morrow sweet lord,
how dost thou sweet lord?' This might be my Lord Such-a-one,   70
that praised my Lord Such-a-one's horse when a meant to beg it,
might it not?

HORATIO Ay my lord.

HAMLET Why, e'en so, and now my Lady Worm's, chopless, and
knocked about the mazard with a sexton's spade. Here's fine   75
revolution, and we had the trick to see't. Did these bones cost no
more the breeding but to play at loggets with 'em? Mine ache to
think on't.

CLOWN   A pickaxe and a spade, a spade,   *Song*
                   For and a shrowding sheet,   80
              Oh a pit of clay for to be made,
                   For such a guest is meet.
                    [*Throws up another skull*]

HAMLET There's another. Why may not that be the skull of a lawyer?
Where be his quiddities now, his quillets, his cases, his tenures, and
his tricks? Why does he suffer this rude knave now to knock him   85
about the sconce with a dirty shovel, and will not tell him of his
action of battery? Hum, this fellow might be in's time a great buyer
of land, with his statutes, his recognizances, his fines, his double
vouchers, his recoveries. Is this the fine of his fines and the recovery
of his recoveries, to have his fine pate full of fine dirt? Will his   90
vouchers vouch him no more of his purchases, and double ones too,
than the length and breadth of a pair of indentures? The very
conveyances of his lands will scarcely lie in this box, and must
th'inheritor himself have no more, ha?

HORATIO Not a jot more my lord.   95

HAMLET Is not parchment made of sheepskins?

HORATIO Ay my lord, and of calves' skins too.

HAMLET They are sheep and calves which seek out assurance in that.
I will speak to this fellow. Whose grave's this sirrah?

CLOWN Mine sir.   100

                         (*Sings*)
              Oh a pit of clay for to be made
                   For such a guest is meet.

HAMLET I think it be thine indeed, for thou liest in't.

CLOWN You lie out on't sir, and therefore 'tis not yours. For my part,
  I do not lie in't, yet it is mine.   105

HAMLET Thou dost lie in't, to be in't and say 'tis thine. 'Tis for the
  dead, not for the quick, therefore thou liest.

CLOWN 'Tis a quick lie sir, 'twill away again from me to you.

HAMLET What man dost thou dig it for?

CLOWN For no man sir.   110

HAMLET What woman then?

CLOWN For none neither.

HAMLET Who is to be buried in't?

CLOWN One that was a woman sir, but rest her soul she's dead.

HAMLET How absolute the knave is! We must speak by the card, or   115
  equivocation will undo us. By the lord, Horatio, this three years
  I have took note of it: the age is grown so picked, that the toe of
  the peasant comes so near the heel of the courtier, he galls his kibe.
  How long hast thou been grave-maker?

CLOWN Of all the days i'th'year, I came to't that day that our last King   120
  Hamlet o'ercame Fortinbras.

HAMLET How long is that since?

CLOWN Cannot you tell that? Every fool can tell that. It was the very
  day that young Hamlet was born, he that is mad and sent into
  England.   125

HAMLET Ay marry, why was he sent into England?

CLOWN Why, because a was mad. A shall recover his wits there, or if
  a do not, 'tis no great matter there.

HAMLET Why?

CLOWN 'Twill not be seen in him there. There the men are as mad as   130
  he.

HAMLET How came he mad?

CLOWN Very strangely they say.

HAMLET How, strangely?

CLOWN Faith, e'en with losing his wits.   135

HAMLET Upon what ground?

CLOWN Why, here in Denmark. I have been sexton here man and boy
  thirty years.

HAMLET How long will a man lie i'th'earth ere he rot?

CLOWN Faith, if a be not rotten before a die, as we have many pocky   140
  corses nowadays that will scarce hold the laying in, a will last you
  some eight year, or nine year. A tanner will last you nine year.

HAMLET Why he more than another?

CLOWN Why sir, his hide is so tanned with his trade, that a will keep
　　　out water a great while, and your water is a sore decayer of your　　145
　　　whoreson dead body. Here's a skull now: this skull hath lien you
　　　i'th'earth three and twenty years.

HAMLET Whose was it?

CLOWN A whoreson mad fellow's it was. Whose do you think it was?

HAMLET Nay I know not.　　　　　　　　　　　　　　　　　　　　　　150

CLOWN A pestilence on him for a mad rogue, a poured a flagon of
　　　Rhenish on my head once. This same skull sir, was Yorick's skull,
　　　the king's jester.

HAMLET This?

CLOWN E'en that.　　　　　　　　　　　　　　　　　　　　　　　　　155

HAMLET Let me see. [*Takes the skull.*] Alas poor Yorick! I knew him
　　　Horatio, a fellow of infinite jest, of most excellent fancy, he hath
　　　borne me on his back a thousand times – and now how abhorred
　　　in my imagination it is! My gorge rises at it. Here hung those lips
　　　that I have kissed I know not how oft. Where be your gibes now?　　160
　　　your gambols, your songs, your flashes of merriment that were wont
　　　to set the table on a roar? Not one now, to mock your own grinning?
　　　Quite chop-fallen? Now get you to my lady's chamber, and tell her,
　　　let her paint an inch thick, to this favour she must come. Make her
　　　laugh at that. – Prithee Horatio, tell me one thing.　　　　　　　165

HORATIO What's that my lord?

HAMLET Dost thou think Alexander looked o' this fashion i'th'earth?

HORATIO E'en so.

HAMLET And smelt so? Pah!　　　　　　　　　　　[*Puts down the skull*]

HORATIO E'en so my lord.　　　　　　　　　　　　　　　　　　　170

HAMLET To what base uses we may return, Horatio! Why may not
　　　imagination trace the noble dust of Alexander, till a find it stopping
　　　a bunghole?

HORATIO 'Twere to consider too curiously to consider so.

HAMLET No faith, not a jot, but to follow him thither with modesty　　175
　　　enough, and likelihood to lead it, as thus: Alexander died, Alexander
　　　was buried, Alexander returneth to dust, the dust is earth, of earth
　　　we make loam, and why of that loam whereto he was converted
　　　might they not stop a beer-barrel?

　　　　　　　Imperious Caesar, dead and turned to clay,　　　　　　180
　　　　　　　Might stop a hole, to keep the wind away.
　　　　　　　Oh that that earth which kept the world in awe
　　　　　　　Should patch a wall t'expel the winter's flaw!
　　　　But soft, but soft! Aside – here comes the king,

The queen, the courtiers.

Enter CLAUDIUS, GERTRUDE, LAERTES, *and a coffin,* [*with* PRIEST] *and* LORDS
attendant

       Who is this they follow?   185
  And with such maimèd rites? This doth betoken
  The corse they follow did with desperate hand
  Fordo it own life. 'Twas of some estate.
  Couch we awhile and mark.   [*Retiring with Horatio*]
LAERTES What ceremony else?   190
HAMLET That is Laertes, a very noble youth. Mark.
LAERTES What ceremony else?
PRIEST Her obsequies have been as far enlarged
  As we have warranty. Her death was doubtful,
  And but that great command o'ersways the order,   195
  She should in ground unsanctified have lodged
  Till the last trumpet. For charitable prayers,
  Shards, flints, and pebbles should be thrown on her.
  Yet here she is allowed her virgin crants,
  Her maiden strewments, and the bringing home   200
  Of bell and burial.
LAERTES Must there no more be done?
PRIEST   No more be done.
  We should profane the service of the dead
  To sing sage requiem and such rest to her
  As to peace-parted souls.
LAERTES   Lay her i'th'earth,   205
  And from her fair and unpolluted flesh
  May violets spring. I tell thee, churlish priest,
  A ministering angel shall my sister be
  When thou liest howling.
HAMLET   What, the fair Ophelia!
GERTRUDE Sweets to the sweet, farewell.   [*Scattering flowers*] 210
  I hoped thou shouldst have been my Hamlet's wife.
  I thought thy bride-bed to have decked, sweet maid,
  And not t'have strewed thy grave.
LAERTES   Oh treble woe
  Fall ten times treble on that cursèd head
  Whose wicked deed thy most ingenious sense   215

Deprived thee of. Hold off the earth awhile
Till I have caught her once more in mine arms.
                          Leaps in the grave
Now pile your dust upon the quick and dead
Till of this flat a mountain you have made
T'o'ertop old Pelion or the skyish head   220
Of blue Olympus.
HAMLET [*Advancing*]   What is he whose grief
Bears such an emphasis? whose phrase of sorrow
Conjures the wandering stars, and makes them stand
Like wonder-wounded hearers? This is I,
Hamlet the Dane.
                  [*Laertes climbs out of the grave*]
LAERTES   The devil take thy soul. [*Grappling with him*]   225
HAMLET Thou pray'st not well.
I prithee take thy fingers from my throat,
For though I am not splenitive and rash,
Yet have I in me something dangerous
Which let thy wisdom fear. Hold off thy hand.   230
CLAUDIUS Pluck them asunder.
GERTRUDE   Hamlet, Hamlet!
ALL   Gentlemen!
HORATIO Good my lord, be quiet.
                  [*The Attendants part them*].
HAMLET Why, I will fight with him upon this theme
Until my eyelids will no longer wag.
GERTRUDE O my son, what theme?   235
HAMLET I loved Ophelia; forty thousand brothers
Could not with all their quantity of love
Make up my sum. What wilt thou do for her?
CLAUDIUS Oh he is mad Laertes.
GERTRUDE For love of God forbear him.   240
HAMLET 'Swounds, show me what thou't do.
Woo't weep, woo't fight, woo't fast, woo't tear thyself?
Woo't drink up eisel, eat a crocodile?
I'll do't. Dost thou come here to whine,
To outface me with leaping in her grave?   245
Be buried quick with her, and so will I.
And if thou prate of mountains, let them throw
Millions of acres on us, till our ground,
Singeing his pate against the burning zone,

                    Make Ossa like a wart. Nay, and thou'lt mouth,   250
                    I'll rant as well as thou.
GERTRUDE   This is mere madness,
                    And thus awhile the fit will work on him;
                    Anon, as patient as the female dove
                    When that her golden couplets are disclosed,
                    His silence will sit drooping.
HAMLET   Hear you sir,   255
                    What is the reason that you use me thus?
                    I loved you ever – but it is no matter.
                    Let Hercules himself do what he may,
                    The cat will mew, and dog will have his day.   *Exit*
CLAUDIUS I pray thee good Horatio wait upon him.   260

                                                          Exit Horatio

                    (*To Laertes*) Strengthen your patience in our last night's
                          speech;
                    We'll put the matter to the present push. –
                    Good Gertrude, set some watch over your son. –
                    This grave shall have a living monument.
                    An hour of quiet shortly shall we see,   265
                    Till then in patience our proceeding be.

                                                              Exeunt

[5.2] *Enter* HAMLET *and* HORATIO

HAMLET So much for this sir, now shall you see the other.
                    You do remember all the circumstance?
HORATIO Remember it my lord!
HAMLET Sir, in my heart there was a kind of fighting
                    That would not let me sleep. Methought I lay   5
                    Worse than the mutines in the bilboes. Rashly,
                    And praised be rashness for it – let us know,
                    Our indiscretion sometime serves us well
                    When our deep plots do pall, and that should learn us
                    There's a divinity that shapes our ends,   10
                    Rough-hew them how we will –
HORATIO   That is most certain.
HAMLET Up from my cabin,
                    My sea-gown scarfed about me, in the dark
                    Groped I to find out them, had my desire,
                    Fingered their packet, and in fine withdrew   15

To mine own room again, making so bold,
My fears forgetting manners, to unseal
Their grand commission; where I found, Horatio –
O royal knavery! – an exact command,
Larded with many several sorts of reasons,   20
Importing Denmark's health, and England's too,
With ho! such bugs and goblins in my life,
That on the supervise, no leisure bated,
No, not to stay the grinding of the axe,
My head should be struck off.

HORATIO   Is't possible?   25

HAMLET Here's the commission, read it at more leisure.
But wilt thou hear now how I did proceed?

HORATIO I beseech you.

HAMLET Being thus benetted round with villainies,
Or I could make a prologue to my brains,   30
They had begun the play. I sat me down,
Devised a new commission, wrote it fair.
I once did hold it, as our statists do,
A baseness to write fair, and laboured much
How to forget that learning; but sir, now   35
It did me yeoman's service. Wilt thou know
Th'effect of what I wrote?

HORATIO   Ay good my lord.

HAMLET An earnest conjuration from the king,
As England was his faithful tributary,
As love between them like the palm might flourish,   40
As peace should still her wheaten garland wear,
And stand a comma 'tween their amities,
And many suchlike as-es of great charge,
That on the view and knowing of these contents,
Without debatement further, more, or less,   45
He should those bearers put to sudden death,
Not shriving time allowed.

HORATIO   How was this sealed?

HAMLET Why, even in that was heaven ordinant.
I had my father's signet in my purse,
Which was the model of that Danish seal;   50
Folded the writ up in the form of th'other,
Subscribed it, gave't th'impression, placed it safely,
The changeling never known. Now, the next day

Was our sea-fight, and what to this was sequent
Thou know'st already. 55

HORATIO So Guildenstern and Rosencrantz go to't.

HAMLET Why man, they did make love to this employment.
They are not near my conscience. Their defeat
Does by their own insinuation grow.
'Tis dangerous when the baser nature comes 60
Between the pass and fell incensèd points
Of mighty opposites.

HORATIO   Why, what a king is this!

HAMLET Does it not, think thee, stand me now upon –
He that hath killed my king, and whored my mother,
Popped in between th'election and my hopes, 65
Thrown out his angle for my proper life,
And with such cozenage – is't not perfect conscience
To quit him with this arm? And is't not to be damned
To let this canker of our nature come
In further evil? 70

HORATIO It must be shortly known to him from England
What is the issue of the business there.

HAMLET It will be short. The interim's mine,
And a man's life's no more than to say 'one'.
But I am very sorry, good Horatio, 75
That to Laertes I forgot myself,
For by the image of my cause, I see
The portraiture of his. I'll court his favours.
But sure the bravery of his grief did put me
Into a towering passion.

HORATIO   Peace, who comes here? 80

Enter young OSRIC

OSRIC Your lordship is right welcome back to Denmark.

HAMLET I humbly thank you sir. – Dost know this water-fly?

HORATIO No my good lord.

HAMLET Thy state is the more gracious, for 'tis a vice to know him.
He hath much land and fertile; let a beast be lord of beasts, and 85
his crib shall stand at the king's mess. 'Tis a chough, but as I say,
spacious in the possession of dirt.

OSRIC Sweet lord, if your lordship were at leisure, I should impart a
thing to you from his majesty.

HAMLET I will receive it sir with all diligence of spirit. Put your bonnet 90 to his right use, 'tis for the head.

OSRIC I thank your lordship, it is very hot.

HAMLET No believe me, 'tis very cold, the wind is northerly.

OSRIC It is indifferent cold my lord, indeed.

HAMLET But yet methinks it is very sultry and hot for my complexion.   95

OSRIC Exceedingly my lord, it is very sultry, as 'twere – I cannot tell
    how. But my lord, his majesty bade me signify to you that a has
    laid a great wager on your head. Sir, this is the matter –

HAMLET I beseech you remember.

[Hamlet moves him to put on his hat]

OSRIC Nay good my lord, for my ease in good faith. Sir, [here is newly   100
    come to court Laertes; believe me an absolute gentleman, full of
    most excellent differences, of very soft society and great showing.
    Indeed, to speak feelingly of him, he is the card or calendar of
    gentry, for you shall find in him the continent of what part a
    gentleman would see.   105

HAMLET Sir, his definement suffers no perdition in you, though I know
    to divide him inventorially would dozy th'arithmetic of memory,
    and yet but yaw neither in respect of his quick sail. But in the verity
    of extolment, I take him to be a soul of great article, and his infusion
    of such dearth and rareness as, to make true diction of him, his   110
    semblable is his mirror, and who else would trace him, his umbrage,
    nothing more.

OSRIC Your lordship speaks most infallibly of him.

HAMLET The concernancy, sir? Why do we wrap the gentleman in our
    more rawer breath?   115

OSRIC Sir?

HORATIO Is't not possible to understand in another tongue? You will
    to't sir, really.

HAMLET What imports the nomination of this gentleman?

OSRIC Of Laertes?   120

HORATIO His purse is empty already, all's golden words are spent.

HAMLET Of him sir.

OSRIC I know you are not ignorant –

HAMLET I would you did sir, yet in faith if you did, it would not much
    approve me. Well sir?]   125

OSRIC You are not ignorant of what excellence Laertes is.

[HAMLET I dare not confess that, lest I should compare with him in
    excellence, but to know a man well were to know himself.

OSRIC I mean sir for his weapon; but in the imputation laid on him
    by them, in his meed he's unfellowed.]   130

HAMLET What's his weapon?

OSRIC Rapier and dagger.

HAMLET That's two of his weapons, but well.

OSRIC The king sir hath wagered with him six Barbary horses, against
the which he has impawned, as I take it, six French rapiers and   135
poniards, with their assigns, as girdle, hangers, and so. Three of
the carriages in faith are very dear to fancy, very responsive to the
hilts, most delicate carriages, and of very liberal conceit.

HAMLET What call you the carriages?

HORATIO I knew you must be edified by the margent ere you had done.   140

OSRIC The carriages sir are the hangers.

HAMLET The phrase would be more germane to the matter if we could
carry a cannon by our sides; I would it might be hangers till then.
But on, six Barbary horses against six French swords, their assigns,
and three liberal-conceited carriages – that's the French bet against   145
the Danish. Why is this impawned, as you call it?

OSRIC The king sir, hath laid sir, that in a dozen passes between yourself
and him, he shall not exceed you three hits. He hath laid on twelve
for nine. And it would come to immediate trial, if your lordship
would vouchsafe the answer.   150

HAMLET How if I answer no?

OSRIC I mean my lord, the opposition of your person in trial.

HAMLET Sir, I will walk here in the hall. If it please his majesty, it is
the breathing time of day with me. Let the foils be brought, the
gentleman willing, and the king hold his purpose, I will win for   155
him and I can. If not, I will gain nothing but my shame and the
odd hits.

OSRIC Shall I redeliver you e'en so?

HAMLET To this effect sir, after what flourish your nature will.

OSRIC I commend my duty to your lordship.   160

HAMLET Yours, yours.

[Exit Osric]

He does well to commend it himself, there are no tongues else for's
turn.

HORATIO This lapwing runs away with the shell on his head.

HAMLET A did comply with his dug before a sucked it. Thus has he,   165
and many more of the same bevy that I know the drossy age dotes
on, only got the tune of the time and outward habit of encounter,
a kind of yesty collection, which carries them through and through
the most fanned and winnowed opinions; and do but blow them
to their trial, the bubbles are out.   170

[*Enter a* LORD

LORD My lord, his majesty commended him to you by young Osric,
who brings back to him that you attend him in the hall. He sends
to know if your pleasure hold to play with Laertes, or that you will
take longer time.

HAMLET I am constant to my purposes, they follow the king's pleasure.   175
If his fitness speaks, mine is ready; now or whensoever, provided
I be so able as now.

LORD The king and queen, and all, are coming down.

HAMLET In happy time.

LORD The queen desires you to use some gentle entertainment to   180
Laertes, before you fall to play.

HAMLET She well instructs me.]

[*Exit Lord*]

HORATIO You will lose, my lord.

HAMLET I do not think so. Since he went into France, I have been in
continual practice; I shall win at the odds. But thou wouldst not   185
think how ill all's here about my heart – but it is no matter

HORATIO Nay good my lord –

HAMLET It is but foolery, but it is such a kind of gaingiving as would
perhaps trouble a woman.

HORATIO If your mind dislike anything, obey it. I will forestall their   190
repair hither, and say you are not fit.

HAMLET Not a whit, we defy augury. There is special providence in
the fall of a sparrow. If it be now, 'tis not to come; if it be not to
come, it will be now; if it be not now, yet it will come – the
readiness is all. Since no man of aught he leaves knows, what is't   195
to leave betimes? Let be.

*A table prepared, with flagons of wine on it. Trumpets, Drums and Officers
with cushions. Enter* CLAUDIUS, GERTRUDE, LAERTES *and* LORDS, *with
other Attendants with foils, daggers and gauntlets*

CLAUDIUS Come Hamlet, come and take this hand from me.

[*Hamlet takes Laertes by the hand*]

HAMLET Give me your pardon sir, I've done you wrong;
But pardon't as you are a gentleman.
This presence knows,   200
And you must needs have heard, how I am punished
With a sore distraction. What I have done,
That might your nature, honour and exception
Roughly awake, I here proclaim was madness.

Was't Hamlet wronged Laertes? Never Hamlet.   205
If Hamlet from himself be tane away,
And when he's not himself does wrong Laertes,
Then Hamlet does it not, Hamlet denies it.
Who does it then? His madness. If't be so,
Hamlet is of the faction that is wronged,   210
His madness is poor Hamlet's enemy.
Sir, in this audience,
Let my disclaiming from a purposed evil
Free me so far in your most generous thoughts,
That I have shot my arrow o'er the house   215
And hurt my brother.

LAERTES   I am satisfied in nature,
Whose motive in this case should stir me most
To my revenge; but in my terms of honour
I stand aloof, and will no reconcilement
Till by some elder masters of known honour   220
I have a voice and precedent of peace
To keep my name ungored. But till that time
I do receive your offered love like love,
And will not wrong it.

HAMLET   I embrace it freely,
And will this brother's wager frankly play.   225
Give us the foils, come on.

LAERTES   Come, one for me.

HAMLET I'll be your foil Laertes. In mine ignorance
Your skill shall like a star i'th'darkest night
Stick fiery off indeed.

LAERTES   You mock me sir.

HAMLET No, by this hand.   230

CLAUDIUS Give them the foils, young Osric. Cousin Hamlet,
You know the wager?

HAMLET   Very well my lord.
Your grace has laid the odds a'th'weaker side.

CLAUDIUS I do not fear it, I have seen you both.
But since he is bettered, we have therefore odds.   235

LAERTES This is too heavy, let me see another.

HAMLET This likes me well. These foils have all a length?

OSRIC Ay my good lord.

Prepare to play

CLAUDIUS Set me the stoups of wine upon that table.

If Hamlet give the first or second hit,   240
Or quit in answer of the third exchange,
Let all the battlements their ordnance fire.
The king shall drink to Hamlet's better breath,
And in the cup an union shall he throw
Richer than that which four successive kings   245
In Denmark's crown have worn. Give me the cups,
And let the kettle to the trumpet speak,
The trumpet to the cannoneer without,
The cannons to the heavens, the heaven to earth,
'Now the king drinks to Hamlet!' Come, begin,   250
And you the judges bear a wary eye.
                           Trumpets the while

HAMLET Come on sir.
LAERTES Come my lord.
                                They play

HAMLET One.
LAERTES No.   255
HAMLET Judgement.
OSRIC A hit, a very palpable hit.
LAERTES Well, again.
CLAUDIUS Stay, give me drink. Hamlet, this pearl is thine.
          Here's to thy health.
               Drum, trumpets sound, and shot goes off
                           Give him the cup.   260
HAMLET I'll play this bout first, set it by awhile.
          Come.
                            [*They play*]
               Another hit. What say you?
LAERTES A touch, a touch, I do confess't.
CLAUDIUS Our son shall win.
GERTRUDE   He's fat and scant of breath.
          Here Hamlet, take my napkin, rub thy brows.   265
          The queen carouses to thy fortune, Hamlet.
HAMLET Good madam.
CLAUDIUS Gertrude, do not drink!
GERTRUDE I will my lord, I pray you pardon me.
                             [*Drinks*]
CLAUDIUS [*Aside*] It is the poisoned cup. It is too late.   270
HAMLET I dare not drink yet madam, by and by.
GERTRUDE Come, let me wipe thy face.

LAERTES My lord, I'll hit him now.
CLAUDIUS   I do not think't.
LAERTES And yet it is almost against my conscience.
HAMLET Come, for the third, Laertes. You do but dally.   275
       I pray you pass with your best violence.
       I am afeard you make a wanton of me.
LAERTES Say you so? Come on.
Play
OSRIC Nothing neither way.
LAERTES Have at you now!   [*Wounds Hamlet*] 280
In scuffling they change rapiers
CLAUDIUS Part them. They are incensed.
HAMLET Nay, come again.   [*Wounds Laertes*]
[*Gertrude falls*]
OSRIC Look to the queen there, ho!
HORATIO They bleed on both sides. How is it my lord?
OSRIC How is't Laertes?   285
LAERTES Why, as a woodcock to mine own springe, Osric.
       I am justly killed with mine own treachery.
HAMLET How does the queen?
CLAUDIUS   She sounds to see them bleed.
GERTRUDE No, no, the drink, the drink – O my dear Hamlet –
       The drink, the drink – I am poisoned.   [*Dies*] 290
HAMLET Oh villainy! – Ho, let the door be locked!
       Treachery! Seek it out!
[*Laertes falls*]
LAERTES It is here Hamlet. Hamlet, thou art slain,
       No medicine in the world can do thee good,
       In thee there is not half an hour of life –   295
       The treacherous instrument is in thy hand,
       Unbated and envenomed. The foul practice
       Hath turned itself on me; lo, here I lie,
       Never to rise again. Thy mother's poisoned –
       I can no more – the king, the king's to blame.   300
HAMLET The point envenomed too! Then, venom, to thy work!
Hurts the king
ALL Treason, treason!
CLAUDIUS Oh yet defend me friends, I am but hurt.
HAMLET Here, thou incestuous, murderous, damnèd Dane,
       Drink off this potion. Is thy union here?   305
       Follow my mother.   *King dies*

LAERTES   He is justly served,
          It is a poison tempered by himself.
          Exchange forgiveness with me, noble Hamlet.
          Mine and my father's death come not upon thee,
          Nor thine on me.   *Dies*   310
HAMLET Heaven make thee free of it! I follow thee.
          I am dead, Horatio. Wretched queen adieu.
          You that look pale, and tremble at this chance,
          That are but mutes or audience to this act,
          Had I but time, as this fell sergeant death   315
          Is strict in his arrest, oh I could tell you –
          But let it be. Horatio, I am dead,
          Thou livest; report me and my cause aright
          To the unsatisfied.
HORATIO   Never believe it.
          I am more an antique Roman than a Dane.   320
          Here's yet some liquor left.
HAMLET   As th'art a man,
          Give me the cup. Let go, by heaven I'll ha't.
          O God, Horatio, what a wounded name,
          Things standing thus unknown, shall live behind me!
          If thou didst ever hold me in thy heart,   325
          Absent thee from felicity awhile,
          And in this harsh world draw thy breath in pain
          To tell my story.
                    March afar off, and shot within
                    What warlike noise is this?
OSRIC Young Fortinbras, with conquest come from Poland,
          To the ambassadors of England gives   330
          This warlike volley.
HAMLET   Oh I die, Horatio,
          The potent poison quite o'ercrows my spirit.
          I cannot live to hear the news from England.
          But I do prophesy th'election lights
          On Fortinbras; he has my dying voice.   335
          So tell him, with th'occurrents more and less
          Which have solicited – the rest is silence.   *Dies*
HORATIO Now cracks a noble heart. Good night sweet prince,
          And flights of angels sing thee to thy rest. –
          Why does the drum come hither?   340

Enter FORTINBRAS *and* ENGLISH AMBASSADORS, *with drum, colours and*
                                    Attendants

FORTINBRAS Where is this sight?
HORATIO   What is it you would see?
        If aught of woe or wonder, cease your search.
FORTINBRAS This quarry cries on havoc. O proud death,
        What feast is toward in thine eternal cell
        That thou so many princes at a shot   345
        So bloodily hast struck?
I AMBASSADOR   The sight is dismal,
        And our affairs from England come too late.
        The ears are senseless that should give us hearing,
        To tell him his commandment is fulfilled,
        That Rosencrantz and Guildenstern are dead.   350
        Where should we have our thanks?
HORATIO   Not from his mouth,
        Had it th'ability of life to thank you;
        He never gave commandment for their death.
        But since, so jump upon this bloody question,
        You from the Polack wars, and you from England,   355
        Are here arrived, give order that these bodies
        High on a stage be placèd to the view,
        And let me speak to th'yet unknowing world
        How these things came about. So shall you hear
        Of carnal, bloody, and unnatural acts,   360
        Of accidental judgements, casual slaughters,
        Of deaths put on by cunning and forced cause,
        And in this upshot, purposes mistook
        Fallen on th'inventors' heads. All this can I
        Truly deliver.
FORTINBRAS   Let us haste to hear it,   365
        And call the noblest to the audience.
        For me, with sorrow I embrace my fortune.
        I have some rights of memory in this kingdom,
        Which now to claim my vantage doth invite me.
HORATIO Of that I shall have also cause to speak,   370
        And from his mouth whose voice will draw on more.
        But let this same be presently performed,
        Even while men's minds are wild, lest more mischance
        On plots and errors happen.

FORTINBRAS   Let four captains
                    Bear Hamlet like a soldier to the stage,   375
                    For he was likely, had he been put on,
                    To have proved most royal; and for his passage,
                    The soldier's music and the rite of war
                    Speak loudly for him.
                    Take up the bodies. Such a sight as this   380
                    Becomes the field, but here shows much amiss.
                    Go bid the soldiers shoot.
                    Exeunt marching, after the which a peal of ordnance are shot off